Sports Makes You Type Faster

OTHER BOOKS BY DAN JENKINS

Novels

Stick a Fork in Me
The Franchise Babe
Slim and None
The Money-Whipped Steer-Job Three-Jack Give-Up Artist
You Gotta Play Hurt
Rude Behavior
Fast Copy
Life Its Ownself
Baja Oklahoma
Limo (with Bud Shrake)
Dead Solid Perfect
Semi-Tough

Nonfiction

Unplayable Lies
His Ownself: a Semi-Memoir
Jenkins at the Majors
Fairways and Greens
"You Call It Sports But I Say It's a Jungle Out There"
I'll Tell You One Thing
Bubba Talks
Saturday's America
The Dogged Victims of Inexorable Fate
The Best 18 Golf Holes in America

SPORTS

Makes You Type Faster

Dan Jenkins | The Entire World of Sports
by One of America's
Most Famous Sportswriters

TCU Press

Fort Worth, Texas

Library of Congress Cataloging–in–Publication Data

Names: Jenkins, Dan, author.
Title: Sports makes you type faster : the entire world of sports by one of
    America›s most famous sportswriters / Dan Jenkins.
Description: Fort Worth, Texas : TCU Press, [2018]
Identifiers: LCCN 2018014004 | ISBN 9780875657011 (alk. paper)
Subjects: LCSH: Sports--United States--Anecdotes. | Sports spectators--United
    States--Anecdotes. | Sportswriters--United States--Anecdotes. | Jenkins,
    Dan. | LCGFT: Sports writing. | Anecdotes.
Classification: LCC GV707 .J48 2018 | DDC 796.0973--dc23
LC record available at
    https://urldefense.proofpoint.com/v2/url?u=https-3A__lccn.loc.gov_2018014004&d=
    DwIFAg&c=7Q-FWLBTAxn3T_E3HWrzGYJrC4RvUoWDrzTlitGRH
    _A&r=O2eiy819IcwTGuw-vrBGiVdmhQxMh2yxeggw9qlTUDE&m=
    SJhYGcUgUEH5YAqC1ZbjR-FmNLuusXzO_-1PNxaP-lY&s=
    r5NIrb-6lp5zrnSsMa5eXXFePcpbacgwcQ9Iewb8sc4&e=

Design by Preston Thomas

TCU Press
TCU Box 298300
Fort Worth, Texas 76129
817.257.7822
www.prs.tcu.edu
To order books: 1.800.826.8911

Always for June, who stepped out of my dreams and brought love to my life. It had to be you.

Wit has truth in it. Jokes are simply calisthenics with words.

—DOROTHY PARKER

If it sounds like writing, I rewrite it.

—ELMORE LEONARD

CONTENTS

PART TWO Individual Games

ABOUT THE AUTHOR

INTRODUCTION

SOMEWHERE ALONG THE WAY when I was trying to decide what to call this book I knew I couldn't go with my working title, *A Mortal Lock and the Hungarian Grip,* which is a piece in here about a ballplayer with a gambling habit. It was too many words. It would break a publishing rule.

Dr. Lorraine Sherley, my creative writing professor at TCU, a sweet lady and a lot of fun for an intellectual, told those of us who aimed to pursue a career in typing for food that a title can never be more than five words. She may have based this on *A Tale of Two Cities,* a novel written a while back by a fellow named Dickens.

I knew she couldn't have based it on anything Proust wrote. You only try to read Proust if somebody has a gun pointed at your head.

Then it was during my senior year that Hemingway's *The Old Man and the Sea* came out to gushing literary acclaim, and I quickly pointed out to Lorraine that the title was *six* words. One too many, right?

To which she said, "But it's Hemingway, isn't it?"

The class laughed. I fondly think of it as the day I took one for the team.

The title I've selected for this work had been sitting here staring at me all along. It was looking at me with affection, like my lovable dog, as opposed to the humorless aunt on my mother's side who was always telling me where to sit.

Sports definitely makes you type faster. Especially if it's a night game or an event on the wrong side of your time zone, or if you work for one of these modern news organizations that demands content and product every thirty minutes—the beast needs to be fed constantly. Quality now lives somewhere near Budapest.

Sportswriting is nothing like writing a novel, where you have time to dwell, contemplate, curse, kick, and drink coffee. Or simply sit and wait for the muse.

Deadlines have been my life since my first day on the *Fort Worth Press* when a wise old ink-stained wretch said, "Kid, stick this in your hat and keep it there. The first obligation of a daily newspaper is to come out every day."

This collection slowly came together over a period of time. Each piece was inspired by a real life occurrence, or a personal experience, or fascination with a historical episode. In an attempt to entertain as well as enlighten, I've hurled humor, satire, farce, and truth at you with intermittent showers of fact. The book deals with all the sports Americans follow. Pro football, college football, golf, basketball, baseball, tennis, prizefighting, track and field, ice hockey, soccer, winter sports, car racing, foxhunting, horse racing, even dining, which today's trendy chefs have turned into a competition. Everything but polo. I thought of having a word about polo but I found out it was invented by Persians.

Overall it concerns itself with the games people play and watch, but it also has its way with those fans who often mistake their favorite sport for a religion.

The vast majority of these pieces are brand-new. But everything in here is new if you consider that the scant few that were previously published have been updated, overhauled, revised, rewritten, and retitled within an inch of their lives.

But only after I took each one to dinner and a movie first.

PART ONE
TEAM SPORTS

After Darrell Royal won two national
Championships with the Wishbone offense
at the University of Texas, he was asked at
a press conference if he was going to keep
the same attack this season, and he replied:
"Like the old gal said at the barn dance,
I'm gonna dance with the one that brung me."

A Word from the Owner

IT DOESN'T seem possible that our football chaps are at it again, but of course this darn cotillion season has kept me hopping.

Well, *that* plus the other distractions you may have read about. Dominique and I *did* run into a bit of difficulty redecorating our second home in Montecito after the forest fire damaged it. Maybe not as much trouble as we encountered a year ago when the blizzard buried our third home in Aspen. The villa in Montecito was something that had to be dealt with immediately. The smoke. The ashes. You can imagine.

There were also the time-consuming debutante balls in New York City, Asheville, Atlanta, Charleston, Birmingham, St. Louis, San Francisco, Boston, Beverly Hills, and Dallas. I thought most of the young ladies were lovely, even if some were a trifle chunky.

I refuse to go as far as Dominique does, complaining that the parties were an endless ordeal of watching fat ducks paddle their way into society.

As for the business at hand, I note that we're only three games into the season. Lot of time for me to catch up.

Not to write my own symphony, but I do find myself in the forefront of the new wave of young NFL owners, and I plan to remain on the cutting edge of what that represents.

Dominique shares my enthusiasm about our team this season. She's giving careful study to improving our halftime entertainment. Without giving anything away, I'll mention only two exciting things: Renaissance choir and modern ballet.

I'm going to make an effort to meet and know as many of you players as possible before the season ends. I already know our quarterback, the exciting Roddy Benoit, or, "You Know It, Benoit," as the media so colorfully refers to him. Roddy escorted one of the debs in Atlanta. The thinnest one, I believe it was.

I do know our charming little placekicker, Raoul Gonzales. He was kind enough to head up the maintenance crew this summer at our family estate in East Hampton. I've told Raoul to hang in there. I'm still working on that citizenship thing for him.

I hope our rookies are blending in with the older fellows. The group includes four of my fraternity buds. I don't apologize for exercising my influence at the draft. Guys who creeped brews with me in the Kap house are more likely than strangers to stand up with me when the going gets tough.

I often reflect back on the things I learned about character, loyalty, and teamwork in my pledge days when the five of us were stripped naked, our heads were shaved, and we were forced to slide down the hallways of barbecue sauce, corn oil, and live minnows.

A word about our new playpen. Ticket sales indicate that we have a loyal fandom. Every ounce as loyal as those who supported the team when my father first moved the franchise from Lackawanna, New York, where it originated, to Grand Forks, North Dakota, which didn't work out—as surveys predicted—and now to Omaha, Nebraska, our headquarters, although the modern, roof-enclosed stadium is located in burgeoning Sioux City, Iowa.

There is no question that some of the players and staff with homes in and around Omaha might be inconvenienced by the ninety-seven-mile drive to Sioux City. But most of our friends with whom Dominique and I have spoken are more than relieved that the league has outlived the unfavorable publicity of recent weeks, such as the bribery of athletes in high school, the exorbitant taxes our fans pay to build our stadiums, our spy network, our signal-stealing devices, and our under-the-table payoffs to potential draft choices and agents. I, for one, have put all that behind me for the cause of patriotism. The NFL is America's game.

I hear that certain fans are less than pleased with our new team colors. Nobody has to remind me of the old black and white Fighting Auk. I have nothing but keen memories of my senior year at Languid Prep. I was the Fighting Auk mascot that season and roamed the sidelines in my costume with the webbed feet and little wings.

Times change and I agree with Dominique that the powder blue and seashell white she chose will have more appeal to the new breed of party-going football fans. Leave it to our grubby opponents to take pride in their Bears, Lions, Tigers, and especially the Buccaneers. A Buccaneer is nothing but a pirate, and Dominique says pirates primarily exist to rob and steal from people like us.

I'm happy with the new logo she designed. I feel that everyone will grow fond of the Auk in his bow tie and top hat.

I hope to attend most of the games the rest of the season, but if business requires my presence elsewhere, you can be sure I will be holding this franchise and all of our merchandising close to my heart.

Oops. I see I have to cut this short. I'm already late for the board meeting at the yacht club.

Go, Auks!

Another Controversy

IF SPORTSWRITERS cherish anything more than a hotel with twenty-four-hour room service, it's a quarterback controversy. It gives them something to write in the middle of the week. What else is there? Injury reports? Quotes from players on what a tough opponent they face coming up? The coach's weekly press conference, which generally provides about as much humor as an autopsy?

But a quarterback controversy attracts readers, lights up the net, and encourages the know-it-alls on sports talk shows to yell at each other louder than they usually do.

The controversy here has a stirring cast of characters. It started with the Lovable Veteran, Casey Culver, and quickly involved Gifted Rookie, Mace McCall, the Conflicted Coach, Butch Mortem, and the Stubborn Owner, Shady Meddling.

The controversy erupted after Casey Culver guided the team to victory in the first two games, then suffered his annual injury. He was replaced by Mace McCall, the Gifted Rookie, who surprisingly won the next eight games in a row, and did it in sparkling fashion.

Coach Butch Mortem said, "Wow, I think we got something here." But the owner called a press conference to set things straight with the media.

Shady Meddling said, "This is still Casey Culver's team. You can't lose your job because of an injury."

A writer spoke up. "You said that last year."

"I did? I'll have to ask my people to check on that."

"You said it the year before. As a matter of fact, you've said it every year for the past five seasons. Casey seems to have a knack for getting injured."

The owner said, "Casey is the most talented quarterback we've had in this franchise. Ask any of our coaches."

"What good is he if he's always sitting on the sideline in street clothes?"

"I'll ignore that comment."

Another writer asked the owner to clarify if Casey's injury is in the shoulder, as it was first thought, or has it moved to the knee, neck, ankle, or elsewhere?

"Our tests are continuing," Shady said. "If we can avoid surgery, he'll be back in the lineup."

The writer said, "How can you justify taking the job away from Mace? He's won eight straight games, thrown thirty-two touchdown passes, and run for more than one thousand yards from scrimmage. His stats are amazing."

The owner said, "We knew he was a good athlete. That's why we drafted him in the twelfth round."

"But you took him as a defensive back."

"We knew he had the tools to play several different positions."

"Most of us are wondering how Mace will react if you take the job away from him . . . give it back to Casey. Is Mace allowed to speak yet?"

"He speaks to me. I can tell you he says he'll do whatever we ask of him if it'll help us get to the playoffs."

"How does Butch feel about this controversy?"

"Coach Mortem knows who pays his salary."

"What about Casey? We haven't heard a word from him. Is he still on his salary of $22 million a year?"

Shady said, "His agent feels strongly that it would create a serious setback on his recovery if his salary were reduced. He backs this up with credible medical advice. As for the rest of your questions, the injury is still giving him trouble with his speech mechanism. We've seen some improvement, but not enough yet."

THE OWNER paused to take out a cigar to chew on. Then somebody asked him if he had given up entirely on the possibility that Casey's problem could be mental.

The owner said, "As you may recall, many theories were tossed around three years ago. That's when we experimented with reincarnation, psychic healing, holistic medicine, mediums, and the occult. None of it helped solve the problem."

"Didn't Satanism play a part?"

"That was two years ago. We tried Satanism along with cosmic isolation, biofeedback, and hypnosis, but to no avail. One more question, then I'm afraid we'll have to go back to getting ready for the Packers."

"Are you finished with the mental testing?"

"Oh, we're nowhere near the point of giving up on that. Right now our people are excited about other possibilities. They're going to try spirit guides, Eastern mysticism, Judeo-Christian rejection, neurolinguistics training, ghost intervention, and we will continue to experiment with— for whatever limited use they're having—drugs."

The Underexposed

DON'T TALK to me about overexposure. I assure you that under my reign as commissioner we haven't begun to explode. I mean, implode. I mean, expand.

Start with the fact that we're sitting here with three evenings in the regular season—Tuesday, Wednesday, Friday—where there are no NFL games on television. Why are we squandering these nights? Why are we letting these millions of Americans mill around bored with their remotes?

Indeed, why should we confine our games to Sunday, Monday, Thursday, and the Saturday after the college season ends?

I'll be attending to this problem soon. Things happen fast these days.

People need to remember that fifty years ago we had only sixteen teams, and everybody in the country was restless. There was a yearning to grow. So today we have thirty-two teams. It could be thirty-six any minute, depending on what I decide to do about the three open cities I have on my hands—St. Louis, Oakland, and San Diego. Applications are already on my desk from the Cuban Gitmos, Nova Scotia Scrunchions, Idaho Spuds, and Martha's Vineyard Lobster Rolls.

The numbers are on the side of expansion.

Consider this. Our current thirty-two teams are located in twenty-three states. Unless my math is wrong this means twenty-seven of these United States do not have an NFL team.

Is that a crime or what?

Moreover, some states are complete hogs. California has three teams—used to have four until Las Vegas stole Oakland. Florida has three. So does New York, unless you want to let New Jersey claim the New York Giants and New York Jets, which I do publicly to avoid riots. The Giants and Jets understand.

Additionally, four other states have two. That would be Texas, Ohio, Pennsylvania, and Maryland. Texas has the Cowboys and Houston, Ohio has the Browns and Bengals, Pennsylvania has the Steelers and Eagles, and Maryland has the Redskins and Ravens, although the *Washington Post* claims the Redskins.

Why is this fair to our nation as a whole?

I look forward to a future when the league will have sixty-four teams in eight divisions with thirty-two of them going to the playoffs, and America able to watch an NFL game seven nights a week.

This could result in starting the regular season in July, or extending it into April. I haven't put the pencil to that yet. But it will be a joy for me to continue the growth of the game. I will have given NFL status to several destitute places.

I'm already taking a closer look at a few previous applicants I'd dismissed out of haste. They look more inviting now. I'm talking about the Oklahoma Frackers, the Oregon Rain, and the Arkansas Walmarts.

My friends know I'm a history nut. So as Admiral Farragut said at the Battle of Mobile Bay, or maybe it was somewhere else, "Lash me to a mast and send me your tired, your poor, your huddled torpedoes—and full speed ahead, I've just begun to fight."

Look, if this job was easy, everybody could do it.

Whose Team
Is It Anyway?

YOU HAVE to concede that the Dallas Cowboys are the most successful innovators in pro football. After all, it was the Dallas franchise that implanted an electronic brain in a mannequin, gave it a snap-brim hat, and assigned it the responsibilities of a head coach.

This is not fair to Tom Landry. I have it on excellent authority that in his record twenty-nine years as coach of the Cowboys, a streak in which he set another NFL record of twenty winning seasons in a row, he is known to have spoken at least ten sentences in public. I personally heard two of them.

Landry's coaching records helped the Cowboys stay in the forefront of America's newsprint and airwaves and reach the zenith of becoming "America's Team." Never mind that they chose that name for themselves.

And they've managed to draw attention to the franchise by hiring employees with enticing nicknames that they either brought with them or earned through their efforts on the field. Many of these nicknames remain lodged in the minds of America:

"Dandy Don" Meredith, Roger "The Dodger" Staubach, Bob "Mr. Cowboy" Lilly, Ed "Too Tall" Jones, Lee Roy "Killer" Jordan, "Bullet Bob" Hayes, Randy "The Manster" White, "TD Tony" Dorsett, Thomas "Hollywood" Henderson, Deion "Prime Time" Sanders, Nate "The Kitchen" Newton, Cliff "Captain Crash" Harris, "The Triplets"—Troy, Emmett, and Michael—not to exclude Chuck Howley and others on the "Doomsday Defense."

Makes you wonder why they didn't think to have an assistant coach named J. R. and a Cowboys cheerleader named Sue Ellen.

Under the ownership of Jerry Jones, the team even proved they could win Super Bowls with two college coaches, Jimmy Johnson and Barry Switzer.

Nobody sneaks ahead of Dallas in blazing trails. We were reminded of this when a Russian troublemaker hacked into their computers recently and shared his findings with the media. The hackers exposed the top prospects Dallas is studying before the next draft. Here are their sure-fire candidates with remarks by members of the scouting department:

Tyree "Spiral Ham" Conway, running back, Alabama.

"This guy is only 5-8, weighs 287. He's a bowling ball. On a single sweep he once crushed nine Vanderbilt tacklers and two officials into the dirt on his way to a touchdown. 'I love the smell of end zones,' he says. 'They smell like . . . victory.'"

Bobby "Bombshell" Grubbs, quarterback, Brazos Technical High School, Frontage Road, Texas.

"This kid will skip college, come straight to the pros. He'll beat out the starter wherever he winds up in the draft. He says, 'I am fleet of foot and my arm is what you call a weapon.' His high school coach says, 'Bombshell is the smartest quarterback I've had here. He made straight As in Fender, Headlight, and Dashboard.'"

Darren "Louver Drape" Barton, defensive end, TCU.

"Darren might be the thinnest player in America at 6-6, 137. But his size works to his advantage. On passing plays, he's a ghost. Hard to find, impossible to grab. An SMU opponent says, 'He's a pass rusher like I've never seen before—when I could find him.'"

Fritsy "Ritzy" Franklin, quarterback, Baylor.

"This kid does it all. Pass, run, lead, and you can add crafty. Coming out of high school in Damp Wind, Washington, Ritzy announced his intention to enroll at Oklahoma State by sitting on the hood of an orange Corvette. Then he announced his intention to enroll at Florida by sitting on the hood of a blue Porsche. Then he announced his intention to enroll at Alabama by sitting on the hood of a red Ferrari. He told me, 'Everybody kept promising a leather interior, but all I saw was velour. Baylor came up big with black leather in the green Jag.'"

Herd "Triple Large" Tyrannosaurus, linebacker, Ohio State.

"It's hard to call Herd a kid. He's 6-7, weighs 390. He don't talk much. More like a growl. His defensive coach said, 'We put Herd in the middle and dared people to throw raw meat at him.' I don't often get this excited about a prospect, but I'm saying Herd Tyranny—he's called that for short—could put some real hurt on the enemies of these United States."

Richie "Trapper" James, cornerback, Oregon Agricultural & Sharing Institute.

"Richie is something of a risk despite his speed, size, and good hands. In the past three seasons he's been caught selling marijuana, shoplifting, and burglarizing a retirement home. He somehow beat all three raps. But you have to like his attitude. He says, 'Look at it this way. I've got so many character flaws there won't be none left for anybody else on the team.'"

Funny Old Cowboys

THE EARLY days of the Dallas Cowboys began with poor little Eddie LeBaron, the original quarterback, trying to see over the line of scrimmage without a stepladder, and tireless Frank Clarke continually racing down the sideline in search of a forward pass that might land in his arms instead dropping at the feet of a soft-drink vendor working the aisle of a yawningly empty Cotton Bowl.

But the team was socially acceptable immediately, thanks to the fondness that the city had for Clint Murchison Jr., Bedford Wynne, and Tex Schramm, and the efforts they made to bring an NFL expansion team to Dallas and paint the territory Cowboy blue.

That color, by the way, wandered through several changes through the years. In the beginning it stirred around somewhere between the baby blue of the University of North Carolina, Dodger blue, royal blue, and what only can be described as Chevrolet blue.

Apart from the owners and executives, it was a brave fan who chose to appear in public in a cashmere blazer of this curious color, a coat that would have been given to him by the Cowboy organization in appreciation of his support.

Full disclosure. I confess that in my newspaper days I was presented with one of those vivid blazers, as were a few other scribes in the area that would become known one day, through no fault of its own, as the Metroplex.

I promptly tucked it away in a closet at home while remarking to my wife, "I'm giving the band a night off."

Those first three seasons from 1960 through 1962 were fun days for the press when the Cowboys competed with Lamar Hunt's Dallas Texans for the favor of football fans and the attention of the press.

It was a millionaire-off. Both Clint and Lamar were great owners, good guys, easy to deal with, and had respect for the printed word.

Their struggle may have peaked one Sunday in the Cotton Bowl when Lamar's Texans—the future Kansas City Chiefs—promoted a game as "Barber's Day." Anyone wearing a white smock was admitted free.

It can hardly be forgotten that the two thousand who showed draped in everything from bedsheets to tablecloths looked less like barbers than they did members of the Klan mingling with dental assistants.

But it was when Dandy Don Meredith took over as the Cowboys' quarterback in 1963 that the true fun and frolic began. There always seemed to be a tug of war going on between the witty and charming Meredith, whose gifted leadership and passing arm often relied on instinct, and the stone-faced man in the hat, Coach Tom Landry, who believed strongly in his wisdom and demanded obedience to his Xs and Os.

The situation may have occasionally caused Landry to reach for the Anacin, but it merely gave Dandy Dan ammunition for humor. He liked to dine out on such exchanges as this one when the coach stood at a blackboard preparing for a game:

LANDRY: "If the Giants do that, we'll do this."
MEREDITH: "What if the Giants don't do that?"
LANDRY: "They will."

But sometimes they didn't. And a large share of the blame for the loss would be heaped on Dandy Dan for having a crucial pass intercepted. This once resulted in Gary Cartwright's immortal lede on deadline in the *Dallas Morning News* in which he gave new life to Grantland Rice's famous words about the Notre Dame backfield.

Wrote Cartwright: "The Four Horsemen rode again Sunday. You know them. Pestilence, Famine, Death, and Meredith."

Of course this bunch of Cowboys would eventually start a trend of winning more games than they lost, having been hammered into shape by Tom Landry's calculus and the offensive fireworks of Dandy Don Meredith, with the help of reliable stalwarts like Don Perkins, Danny Reeves, Bob Hayes, and Ralph Neely, not to overlook the defensive heroics of Bob Lilly, Chuck Howley, Lee Roy Jordan, and Mel Renfro.

They were the most prominent pioneers of the future dynasty.

It might also be remembered that by 1966 the Cowboy uniforms had happily progressed from a goofy blue and white to a sensible blue and silver.

Predictably, it was left to Dandy Don to have the last word on that entertaining era.

"Tom Landry was a perfectionist," he said. "If he was married to Raquel Welch, he'd expect her to cook."

The Patriot

EVERYBODY KNOWS I'm a football hero, the idol of kids, a role model in the community. But I'd been feeling like I needed something else to cement my legend. Something patriotic. That's why I got interested when my girlfriend suggested I bring back the fad of burning American flags and refusing to stand for the national anthem at every opportunity.

I told her I remembered how it had once been an interesting thing to do, but I wasn't sure it would attract any attention now.

She insisted it would—there was a new sense of patriotism in the air.

My girlfriend is a looker. Well, she is when you get around the garb. She's a brunette under the head thing. She was born Brenda Jane Anderson, but in college she was becoming a more intelligent person and changed her name to Abida Yousef because it fit her adopted religion.

This was after Abida became enlightened by a young professor who had a lasting influence on her worldview. He gave mesmerizing lectures. His name was Dr. Hamman Majeed, but recently he'd gone back to his birth name of Billy Jack Christopher. It was either make the change or be cut out of his father's will.

Abida is smarter than me. I only went to JC. When I said to her that burning flags and not standing for the anthem could look like treason to most people, Abida said, "No longer. Nothing is treasonous in America now. Higher education has opened our minds to expanded horizons."

I said, "Boy, my seventh grade teacher sure had things wrong."

Abida said, "Have you ever seen one of your political leaders go to prison for lying, cheating, stealing, sabotage, anything? Never. They start learning the rules of the game the minute they go to work in Washington, DC. Prison is for stupid people."

"You could be right."

She said, "I *am* right. Have another dish of the goat brains I fixed. They're good for you."

I said, "I'm too full. But I will have another cup of that Turkish coffee."

Abida said, "I know you just want to make a statement. You don't want to participate in the protests or shopping."

"Shopping?"

"It used to be called looting. But the media has rightly decided that the term is unfair to certain groups in our society."

I said, "I've seen TV shows about the student protests in the sixties. College kids yelling, shutting down the campus, smoking dope. Must have been fun."

"Ancient history," Abida said. "Protests are different now. Activists are more motivated today. In the region from which I've taken my name, if the cause is serious enough, the activists blow up people in public places with bombs. Often themselves."

"They blow up innocent people?"

"There are no innocent people in this world."

I THOUGHT I should ask the commissioner if it was okay to protest something again? When they put me through to him, he sounded irritable.

He said, "This isn't about concussions, is it?"

He was relieved when I said no, it was about the rules. Was there anything new in the rules that said I couldn't burn an American flag or take a knee during the anthem?

"Why do you want to bring this up again? We had enough trouble with it the first time around. I stand by my previous statements. The league believes in freedom of speech and expression. Up to a point. Depending. Sort of."

I said, "My girlfriend suggested it. Her name is Abida Yousef."

"Where did you meet this young lady?"

"It's kind of funny," I said. "I tripped over her in the lobby of a movie tavern. She was down on her knees, bent over on the carpet. I spilled a plate of nachos on her."

The commissioner said go ahead and express myself, but try not to drag the whole team or any advertisers with me.

I was psyched for our next road game. I was first off the team bus when we arrived at the stadium in Dallas. I carried an American flag with me and jogged over to a group of fans who were tailgating. I'd never seen candelabra on a table with barbecue ribs before.

I asked around, "Who wants to join me in an act of patriotism?"

I spread the flag out on the ground and stomped on it while three people stared at me and the others kept eating ribs. I took out a Bic lighter and set fire to the flag and started moonwalking around it.

What happened next is still a blur. I woke up in a hospital room with an arm and a leg in a cast and a brace around my neck. Abida was sitting in a chair by my bed reading a book with scratch marks in it as opposed to, you know, words.

She looked at me and said, "You made me proud today."

I said, "Yeah, well, I just wish I'd known that there weren't that many patriots in Texas."

You Talking to Me?

IT'S NOT that I want to see football dragged back to leather helmets, long-sleeve wool jerseys, canvas pants, and high-top shoes, but the time has come when so-called progress needs to have its throat stepped on.

A good start would be to rip the mic out of every pro quarterback's helmet.

I've been privileged to know many illustrious quarterbacks in the past. Guys like Sam Baugh, Bobby Layne, Sonny Jurgensen, others of prominence. They accepted a play from the sideline on occasion, but they could not imagine anybody regularly calling plays for them. In fact, Bobby Layne once told me that if a person *did* try to call plays for him, he would have asked Joe Schmidt to turn the guy into a casserole. Yet those quarterbacks managed to be successful.

And I don't hesitate for a moment to give extra credit to Tom Brady of the Patriots for winning a handful of Super Bowls while listening in his helmet to a voice saying, "Sorry about the interruption, Tom, but it's looking like a quick toss to the tight end instead of a pitchout to the other side. By the way, how was dinner last night at *L'Espalier*? Up to standards?"

But since the mic went in the helmet I've been fearing the day when every pro team will dress its players in leotards, muscle shirts, deck shoes, and skullcaps. Oh, and the league will rule tackling below the waist a penalty.

Except the quarterback won't be wearing a skullcap. He'll be wearing an advanced combat headset with which he'll be able to tap into conversations of our foreign enemies, or switch over to a Harry Connick Jr. album, if he doesn't like the play that's sent in by his offensive coordinator, who will be circling over the stadium in a Citation X.

As for the future of uniforms, it's hard to imagine the pro game's early stars like Bronko Nagurski, Ken Strong, or Dutch Clark, dressed in leotards and muscle shirts. If so, they wouldn't be playing football for a living. They'd be living in Santa Fe making pottery.

But it's a new world. The players are rich, the owners are richer, and people are reading fake news on devices held in their palms. None of us could have guessed that football was going to be played solely for the pleasure of the occupants of luxury boxes.

Young fans scoff today when I try to tell them that NFL teams once played outdoors in baseball parks, and most of the original owners were bookmakers whose major concern was the rising cost of towels.

OWNERS AND PLAYERS today have grown wealthier than they could have dreamed through TV and marketing schemes, so it's not surprising that many of my fellow writers have become preoccupied with money in their stories.

You may have read a story like this:

"The Eagles' Squishy Fielder, who will earn $12 million this season not including bonuses, intercepted a pass from the New York Giants and returned it 34 yards for the winning touchdown yesterday. The pass was thrown by Hasty Cameron, who may have been worrying about the infringement clauses in his licensing agreements, according to his agent, Snapper Sampson.

"The agent said Hasty was also concerned about a rumor that the new owner of the Giants, Laddy Winthrop III, was demanding that taxpayers build him a $170 billion dollar stadium in Times Square with a seating capacity of 500,000 or he will move the franchise to an island in the Netherlands Antilles."

Technology being what it is, there will come a time when the fan at home will be able to listen in on a conversation between the quarterback and the running back. The fan will hear:

"Curtis, good buddy, I'd like to consider a sweep, but you will have to discharge your obligation as a self-employed individual, including all trademarks, trade names, and copyrights."

"You talking to me?"

"Yes. Aren't you my squirty little dipsy-doodle ball-carrier? I'm not clear as to what happens in the case of an audible, particularly if the play results in presenting you in a bad light, or embarrassing you, or damaging your reputation as a running back."

"You're talking to me, right?"

"Please, I can barely hear as it is. I'm obligated to remind you that you will agree to furnish a touchdown of any length from this scrimmage line, and you have no right to privacy in this endeavor. You may be held responsible to indemnify our head coach, general manager, or owner for any loss of yardage or damages plus any and all legal fees in the event that you are unsuccessful."

"You still talking to me?"

"Shut up, dang it! Where was I? Is somebody speaking Russian to me? Guess not. Okay. I'm finally obligated to tell you that this assumes no person, firm, or corporation will interfere with your performance. All that said, you may want to consult your attorney before the snap."

The Zebra Follies

PRO FOOTBALL'S REPLAY OFFICIAL, the "electronic zebra," who sits upstairs in the stadium and decides the fate of the world, inspires a TV series that would send a network's ratings through the roof of a domed stadium, if not through the top of a sportscaster's ego.

In the pilot episode, a fumble is scooped up by a defensive player who carries it into the end zone for a touchdown. Two zebras signal a score, but two others throw their flags.

The referee calls a meeting.

In real life, you can't hear what goes on in these meetings, but that's the charm of the TV show.

We watch the ref say to the umpire, "What have we got, Charley?"

"Touchdown, defense."

The ref turns to Eddie, the back judge.

"No touchdown," the back judge says. "The guy was down."

The ref calls in the field judge. "How'd you see it, Fritz?"

"See what?"

"The play. Fumble or no fumble?"

"Frank, I don't know. I was watching the Dallas cheerleaders. Hot."

"We better ask upstairs," says the ref.

Gavin, the replay official, is sipping champagne and spreading caviar on a bite of party rye when he hears, "It's Frank on the field, Gavin."

"I hear you," Gavin says. "What is it *this* time?"

The ref says, "How do you see the play?"

"The field goal was good."

"What field goal?"

"The one the Dolphins kicked."

"What game are you watching, Gavin?"

"Dolphins-Broncos. What game do you think I'm watching?"

"Well," the ref says, "we were sort of hoping it was the Cowboys-Giants."

"All anybody has to do is *tell* me."

Down on the field, the referee again addresses the back judge.

"Eddie, are you sure it wasn't a fumble?"

"The ground can't cause a fumble."

"Wait a darn minute," says the ref. "You're telling *me*, a man who's worked *eight* Super Bowls, that when a ball-carrier is tackled, hits the ground, and loses the football . . . that's *not* a fumble?"

"Frank, the ground can't cause a fumble."

"Well, that's the gallderndist thing I've ever heard," the ref says. "Back when I played, the ground was the main thing that *could* cause a fumble."

The head linesman asks for calm.

"Gentlemen," he says, "we should consider what a touchdown would do at this point. It would put the Cowboys up by fourteen and a half. Is that really what we want?"

The umpire steps in again.

"Good point," he says. "My next door neighbor has the Giants and ten. Right now, he's ahead. He's a great guy with a nice family. I don't want to sway anybody, but he's hoping to buy his wife a new Samsung fridge with an ice cube dispenser for her birthday. This game could do it for him."

"Oh, really?" the back judge says. "Well, my next door neighbor is a great guy too. Me and him have the Under today and I'd like to sew it up."

The referee says, "I'm going to pretend I didn't hear any of this. . . . Gavin, is that you on the line?"

Gavin says, "Frank, I've looked at the replay five times."

"Good. What do you see?"

"I can't tell."

"You *can't tell?* Jesus, Gavin. It's your *job.*"

"Don't snap at me, Frank. I've looked at it from every angle. I think you can call it a fumble if you like, but I think you can get away with calling it no fumble. It's up to you."

"Listen to me, Gavin. You're calling it no fumble. The ground can't cause a fumble."

"Since when?"

"Just do what I say, okay?"

"Hey, whatever, Frank. You da man."

The episode ends as Gavin takes a sip of champagne and switches his TV over to the Discovery Channel to watch a tuna boat fight its way through a storm.

What's in a Name?

VICTIMHOOD, a fad that keeps gripping America, reached a crescendo for me halfway into the millennium when an individual pretended to topple over in agony after discovering that the mascot of the Washington Redskins for the past eighty years was, in fact, a redskin.

The individual was rumored to be a one sixty-fourth Native American. He became severely distressed by this discovery, so he let his feelings be known as loudly as possible when there was a TV camera on a street corner.

It enabled him to round up a small group of other one sixty-fourth Native Americans to join his protest after they consulted a dictionary and—this is just a guess—looked up the word reparation.

Their efforts turned this into a burning issue for newspapers, Facebookers, bloggers, cable channels, and every fake news outlet in America that enjoys alarming our citizens about NFL mascots and other threats to society, like, oh, hurricanes, terrorism, nuclear catastrophes, what have you.

Fortunately for the sensible among us, these alarmists and self-styled victims took it on the chin four years later. It happened when the Supreme Court of the United States, in the interest of free speech, issued a unanimous ruling essentially saying that the Redskins could continue to be Washington's mascot.

This meant that the Cleveland Indians, Kansas City Chiefs, and Florida State Seminoles could breathe easier. And the Stanford Indians and Dartmouth Indians could come back from wherever they'd been. The enemies of free speech had finally lost a battle.

The ruling was a cause to celebrate for those of us raised in a free country. It was fun to see the professional victims take a hit for a change.

They'd been on a long win streak, thanks to a glut of misguided souls in the teaching profession and help from the politically correct media.

Not that the threats to the NFL are over. Victims in our society are a fragile clan. At the mere mention of a certain mascot, they're capable of dropping like flies, or even totem poles.

Therefore, as a civic duty I've prepared a number of solutions for trouble spots that are likely to turn up in the future.

We can do away with the Cowboys in Dallas. Cowboys are cruel to horses, and horse lovers have made a slight headway by publicly accusing cowboys of torturing horses with spurs and whips. Cowboys make horses gallop, trot, canter, jump, and buck when a horse only wants to stand, chew, and whinny.

Rename them the Dallas Ranchers. A rancher is harmless. All he does is sit in a chair on the porch of his homestead and wait for somebody to discover oil on the property.

The New York Giants have long been a problem. Activists argue that Giants primarily appeal to people six feet five and over. I say call them the New York Ordinary Average Vertically Limited Passport-Challenged Multicultural Diversified Transgender Inclusives. Cover all the bases.

The Saints of New Orleans struck me as a poorly chosen mascot from the start. The fact is, there are only ten thousand official church-declared saints in the world, not counting Meryl Streep and Barbra Streisand, who ordained themselves.

That's hardly enough to fill a stadium. A Saint is obviously offensive to atheists, who are people too, although most of them missed the meeting at which it was determined that there are no atheists in a foxhole.

Make them the New Orleans Beignets. Maybe Fritters or Pastries works better if you have trouble pronouncing beignet. Granted, it's a challenge.

For a while now, the San Francisco 49ers have been in need of a new mascot. The 49ers were people who joined the California Gold Rush of 1849. That is so yesterday, as the coeds say. Or used to.

People in the City by the Bay are likely to embrace the team with more pride if they become the San Francisco Hippies, Druggies, Weed, or Libs.

No NFL franchise has been more clumsily named than the Buffalo Bills. The logo resembles a bison, but the nickname is based on Buffalo Bill Cody, the frontiersman, who lived his life in places as far away from Buffalo, New York, as possible. Wyoming, for instance.

You could argue that other characters of the Old West were as popular as the buffalo hunter and are entitled to have their names attached to a franchise. Why should we ignore Wild Bill Hickok, Kit Carson, Wyatt Earp, Calamity Jane, Annie Oakley, Billy the Kid, Jesse James, and John Wayne?

It would have made better sense if the citizens had chosen to be the Buffalo Falls. Niagara is only seventeen miles from Buffalo. What were these people thinking?

Nothing else needs protection at the moment. Even in Pittsburgh and Green Bay. Steeler fans continue to take pride in their city that once had 4,567 steel mills. Today they still wear their hard hats at jaunty angles, and with dignity.

Likewise, Packer fans. They take pride in wearing blocks of cheese on their heads. What this has to do with packing Vienna sausages and corned beef hash into cans, I have yet to understand.

These are only suggestions. All I want is a more peaceful world.

The Big Game

THERE WAS ONCE a more romantic time in our lives when the college football hero strived to excel because of his love for the girl next door, who wore saddle oxfords, a pleated skirt, his letter sweater, and bore an uncanny resemblance to a young Teresa Wright.

Movies were made of those days. Remember?

Curly Stalwart, State's star quarterback and all-around good person, is kidnapped by some unshaven gangsters on the eve of the big game between State and Normal.

Nothing in sports compares to the rivalry between State and Normal. It has broken up families, friendships, pitted brother against brother.

Woe is the coach of State, Goldie Nails, who is tough as nails but has a heart of gold.

Coach Nails races to see Shirley Sue, Curly's girlfriend, who happens to be the sweetheart of Sigma Chi and lives in a little house with a white picket fence not far from Flirtation Walk.

"Curly's been kidnapped," the coach says to Shirley Sue, who is helping her mother bake a cake.

"No!" Shirley Sue cries out, dropping the mixing bowl. "We can't win the big game against Normal without Curly!"

The coach says, "I don't know what to do, Shirley Sue. They'll be kicking off soon—I should be at the stadium."

Shirley Sue says, "I know what to do. Bozo and I will find Curly and rescue him. I suspect those unshaven gangsters we've seen around town are holding Curly hostage in the haunted house near Lookout Point. They must have a big bet on Normal."

"Could be," the coach says, rushing out the door.

Bozo is Shirley Sue and Curly's best friend. A pudgy kid who makes funny faces to entertain friends when he's not playing clarinet in the swing band he organized with Huck, Skinny, Stormy, and Bags. They jam when everybody dances at the malt shop.

Shirley Sue drives her jalopy to the malt shop. Bozo hops in and they speed to the haunted house. Bozo distracts the unshaven gangsters by playing the "Washington and Lee Swing" on his clarinet while Shirley Sue hastily unties Curly from a chair and removes his blindfold.

"Don't worry about me," Bozo hollers. "Get Curly to the game!"

"Bozo's a good egg," Curly says, as Shirley Sue speeds back through town, weaving in and out of men who wear suits and hats and women who wear pearls and gloves. "Bozo is so swell," Shirley Sue says.

They arrive at the stadium as the fourth quarter starts. State trails Normal by seventeen points. Three touchdowns will do it for State. Curly says, "I'm going to win this game for you, Shirley Sue."

"No, Curly," she says, kissing him on the cheek. "You're going to win it for everybody who believes in love . . . friendship . . . loyalty . . . and America!"

On the sideline, Curly slips into his football uniform. Shirley Sue slips into her cheerleader costume. Curly trots onto the field. The crowd roars.

State lines up in the Notre Dame box formation. Curly says, "Forty-two, twenty-three, sixteen . . . hike!"

Curly dashes seventy-four yards for a touchdown. State gets the ball back.

Curly says, "Sixty-two, nineteen, twenty-four, hike!" Curly sprints eighty-eight yards for a touchdown.

Under the unique rules of the era, a team gets the ball back every time it scores a touchdown. Now State is backed up on its own one-yard line after an unfair penalty called by an unshaven referee. There are only five seconds left to play and State is ninety-nine yards away from pay dirt. Woe is State.

In the huddle, Curly looks at his teammates and says, "This is it, fellows. I say we take a shot with KF-79 . . . on two."

Fatty Barnes, a tackle, says, "I'll block three guys for you, Curly."

Curly takes the snap, throws a pass to himself, runs thirty yards, pitches a lateral to himself, and scoots into the end zone for the winning touchdown.

Ecstatic fans swarm the field. They carry Curly and Shirley Sue all the way to the malt shop, where Bozo, his head bandaged, is playing the clarinet and leading the swing band in a rendition of "You Gotta be a Football Hero (to Get Along with the Beautiful Girls)."

Huck is on trombone, Skinny on drums, Bags on bass, Stormy on

Trumpet, and Coach Goldie Nails sits in on piano. Kids are doing the Lindy Hop. Over at a corner table, Curly and Shirley Sue sip on separate straws from a chocolate malt.

"I love America," Curly says.

"And I love you," says Shirley Sue. "Isn't life grand?"

THINGS ARE DIFFERENT these days.

When State's star quarterback Dead-Eye Thurber tests positive for thermozoom and steroidazine on the eve of the big game against Normal, Dead-Eye's girlfriend, Amber Tattoo, cranks up the Porsche her daddy gave her for reining in her back-talk. She drives to the football compound, which is fifteen miles from the State campus and consists of plush condos, indoor and outdoor swimming pools, tennis courts, an eighteen-hole golf course, bowling alley, billiard parlor, trout stream, five-star restaurant, pub, movie theater, and pharmacy.

Amber tracks down Bobby Chyron in his suite. Bobby Chyron is State's All-America halfback. He is stretched out in bed.

"Dead-Eye's tested positive," Amber says. "He'll miss the big game."

"Better him than me," Bobby says, reaching to a table and picking up a joint the size of his forearm. "Want to burn one?"

Amber Tattoo says, "Oh, I guess I have an hour or two to spare."

She lights up.

Two hours later, Amber wanders around aimlessly but finds Rusty Hammer, State's All-America linebacker. He's in the players' pub stirring up a batch of margaritas.

"Dead-Eye's tested positive," Amber mumbles. "He's out of the big game against Normal. What are we gonna do?"

Rusty says, "I don't know about you, but I'm gonna put Normal in a three-team parlay with Ohio State and LSU. Here, try some of this."

Amber washes down three amphetamines with two goblets of margaritas and does four lines of coke. Rusty does the same.

"What do you want to do now?" Rusty asks.

Amber says, "Aw, screw the game. Grab your guns and ammo. We'll suck up some more rocket fuel, hop in my Porsche, and go kill somebody for fun."

Minutes later, howling with laughter, they speed away.

The Savior

GENTLEMEN, let me just say up front that in every coaching job I've held I've never had a reception like this from a Board of Regents. If your enthusiasm carries over into the season, we're gonna win our share of football games. Now I know some of you sitting here will translate that into which one of you rich guys is gonna buy me that running back I want over in Possum Trot, Texas?

Figured I'd get a laugh with that. Good icebreaker.

I want to make it clear that in all the years I've spent in this game I've never backed off from a challenge, big or small. Of course I prefer the small ones. Those big ones can get you fired. Heh, heh.

I want these kids to think of me as their father. If they have a personal problem, I want 'em to come to me first.

What's that, Roy? Until their eligibility is up, you said? I knew there'd be a wise guy in the crowd.

Most of you know these kids I've inherited were pretty good football players at one time. You probably wonder what happened to 'em. I'll tell you what happened. The film I've seen tells me that the guy I've replaced here couldn't coach a team of fat boys in a pizza-eating contest.

If you want my overall view of this game, I personally think it's time for college coaches to realize we're in the entertainment business. That's why I'm determined to open up this offense. But that's not to say I won't yank the chain on my first quarterback who throws a pass from inside our own twenty.

I can't stress too strongly that our kids are here to receive an education first and play football second. Nevertheless, I hope you people know you'll have to bend a rule or two if you want me to get the job done, not that what I say here should leave this room.

Another thing I want to make clear. You will never hear me criticize the game officials in public. They have a difficult job and they'll sometimes make honest mistakes. But I'm only human. If one of those douchebags costs us a win with a criminal call, I'll tell him to his face he's a cheating pile of elephant dung and I hope he dies screaming at his innards.

Thanks. I appreciate the applause.

Finally, I want y'all to know I understand that the media has a job to do. That's why as a head coach I've always tried to be cooperative with the sportswriters and broadcasters.

But I'll let you in on this. I've already tangled with one particular writer in this town. And if he don't get off my butt, it won't grieve me to find out that his wife and kids have contracted an incurable disease.

Sorry I can't stay for lunch. Got a kid waiting in my office. He's that 330-pound, six-foot-six offensive tackle everybody's been after. He'll be the key to the vault for us. I want to thank whoever it was in this room that sprung for his Mercedes-Benz S650, the house for his family, and arranged the vice president's job for his daddy at Lakeside Bank & Trust.

That's the kind of loyalty that'll put this university in the national playoffs someday soon. There's an old saying where I come from, and I lived by it my whole life. It ain't braggin' if you can do it, and it ain't flattery if it's true.

Red Dog's Diary

THROUGH MY FRIENDSHIP with Red Dog Hawkins I have come in possession of a diary he kept in his last season as the head recruiter at Lord Jesus University, or LJU, as the school prefers to be known. That's since the unfortunate scandal in which twenty-two members of the football team were accused of allegedly gang-raping seventy-eights coeds on the campus. The investigation is still ongoing.

You may know that Red Dog has left LJU to accept a job with a waste management company at Disney World in Orlando. We wish him well.

He handed over his diary to me in the hope that I will print parts of it in this newspaper as proof that LJU operated no differently in its recruiting practices than any other university among the major conferences.

That's what I'm doing today, and I believe the exposure will be for the good of the great American game we all love. If this results in my winning a journalism award, that can't be helped.

Here are Red Dog's entries that I find the most revealing:

"JAN. 10. Time to make the big move on Tank Mitchell. This kid can keep our train on the track. We haven't had anyone this big and powerful since Tip-Toe Allen left high school in time to lead us to the Cotton Bowl.

"The kid will do anything you ask of him. If I say, 'Tank, I want you to go over to Egypt and knock down them pyramids,' he'll do it. Character is what I'm talking about. You can't teach it.

"I'm taking Tank to dinner tonight with his two kid brothers, Truck and Crane. They're still in high school. They're good prospects and could follow him to our campus.

"JAN. 11. We have trouble. Tank came to dinner at the Dairy Queen with his brothers in a new Cadillac SUV. I asked where he got it. He said,

'I'm not at liberty to say.' I asked if he got it from Oklahoma, Florida State, or Clemson?

"He said, 'I definitely didn't get it from Oklahoma, Florida State or Clemson.'

"I said, 'Did you get it from anybody in the SEC?'

"He said, 'I'm not at liberty to say.'

"JAN. 16. I went to Coach Bull Cooper and told him we needed to put Mr. McConnell on the case. That's B. L. 'Big Load' McConnell, who took rich in the oil and gas business.

"Big Load played ball for LJU and he will do whatever it takes to keep our engine running. He built us the new stadium and apartment complex for the football scholars. He loves to entertain the coaches with trips on his private jets and fleet of yachts.

"I let Big Load know we were having trouble signing Tank. He said, 'Hell, that ain't nothing we can't fix by taking him on a cruise with a passel of fun-loving ladies.'

"JAN. 23. It was a good trip. Tank thinks he's leaning toward LJU now with one week to go before signing day. He'd never seen an ocean before until we stepped off Big Load's Gulfstream onto his private island where his biggest yacht is docked. Tank looked at the blue water of the Bahamas and asked me if this was the same ocean our United States Navy floated on. I said I was sure part of it was.

"FEB. 2. I felt like we needed two more clinchers to sign Tank. I brought in the chancellor first. He guaranteed Tank that he wouldn't have to attend any classes to make his grades, either during football season or in the spring. Tank said, 'That's good because my brain needs to rest when I'm not toting the leather into the end zones of my choice.'

"When Tank asked for $200,000 a year for four years, it could have been a deal-breaker. But Big Load took care of it. The Church of Ezekiel across the street from the LJU campus is still affiliated with the school despite the rape scandal. Big Load suggested he donate Tank's money to the church, and the preachers could deal out the payments to Tank. The chancellor and Coach Cooper said they didn't hear this conversation, but it sounded like a good idea.

"FEB. 4. This is a happy day for me as a recruiter. Tank Mitchell signed his National Letter of Intent with us, and it's great to know that Lord Jesus University's football future is still in the hands of God."

A Cry in the Dark

IN CASE you've never been in my current position in your own life, let me assure you it's not easy to go from being the center of the universe to a fired college football coach. A fired coach, I might add, that people would rather see sitting in jail eating a baloney sandwich than pretend they know him now.

That's me. The man who rescued this university from the garbage dump. It had been looking sorry for twenty years because the dim-witted administration was wasting its money on electron microscopes, professors who speak unknown tongues, and building intramural fields for sissies.

I took the school to eight straight bowl games, and I did it with nothing but my brains and a little financial help from rich alums who'd grown tired of their university looking like a cow patty on a platter of prime New York strips.

And what was my reward? The administration goes into raging fits over four incidents that the no-count media turns into a series of terrorist attacks tied in with rumors of a serial rapist running loose on the campus.

I want to thank you folks for giving me the opportunity to tell my side of the story. This might be the last time I speak in public until I land another coaching job. I've had nibbles from two high schools in West Texas. So my future looks a little brighter than a case of the crabs.

I'll address the problems that came up in the order in which they caused me to cuss academic drones out loud to their faces and beards.

TOMMY TED BROTHERS was a good kid in every way you wanted to measure him. He could find an end zone like I've never seen. It was a rare thing if one defender brought him down. He left a covey of linebackers calling nine-one-one after they tried to meet him head-on.

I didn't want to believe a word of the girl's testimony. Things happen when two people are scuffling around, and sometimes those things can be misconstrued. I figured she was in it for the money. She knew he was gonna be a high draft pick.

At first I didn't want to believe the business about Tommy Ted taking a bite out of her neck. But I'm willing to shoulder part of the blame for that now. I should have delved deeper into his background when we were recruiting him. I like to think I'd have handled him differently if I'd known his nickname in high school was "Dracula."

JIMMY SLATER was never known for his patience. We knew this. He was a first-rate cornerback, but too often he went for the interception and gave up six. He compensated for it in other ways. Good kick returner, strong defender against the run. But his lack of patience eventually got him in trouble.

Fast-food places pissed him off. They'd always get his order wrong at the drive-through. It didn't matter whether it was a Mac's or some other establishment. If he asked for two cheeseburgers, large fries, and a Coke, he'd wind up with one burger, two fries, and no Coke, but he'd speed away before he discovered it. He tried teaching himself to talk slower and enunciate better, but it didn't make any difference.

One day at Burger Bob's they got his order right. It was a miracle. But the woman at the window couldn't make change for five dollars. He waited and waited and eventually slid out of his car and crawled into the window and grabbed her by the throat, but he got stuck in the pay widow.

When the police arrived, Jimmy's legs were flapping outside the window and inside the restaurant his hands were around the woman's neck while other employees were beating on him with utensils and their fists to turn her loose.

Jimmy was arrested for aggravated assault. It didn't help that the town came to his defense, if you remember. Everybody said they understood his frustration. It was unfortunate that the media raised such a fuss about it that I was forced to dismiss him from the team. As far as I'm concerned, that was one more example of the press not having its priorities straight.

I don't have any idea where Jimmy is now, but I know one thing. Wherever it is, he's not taking any lip.

I STILL MAINTAIN it wasn't right for the university to hire a stove-hot lady professor who wore skin-tight jeans, high heels, and low-cut blouses. I'm talking about Dr. Heather Scott. Women professors are supposed to wear smocks and look like prison matrons, aren't they? They did in my day.

Dr. Scott taught a history course about the Vietnam War. She called it, "Dinks in the Wire." All my players wanted to enroll in the course, but she only accepted two of them—our starting quarterback, Buddy Monroe, and our tight end, Clipper Bailey.

It should have been a warning when she frequently invited Buddy and Clipper over to her apartment for dinners and tutoring.

I refuse to accept the story that she was gang-banged by my kids. The kids say she did it to *them*, one after the other, and bruised her own face with her fists. I hated it when the university settled with her out of court for five million bucks, mainly to chase the scandal out of the media.

I'm convinced it was a scam. Heather Scott has her own TV show now, plus a book deal. No wonder she gave up teaching. Buddy and Clipper were kicked out of school. Consequently we suffered an embarrassing loss in the Mango Bowl to Louisiana Tech, if you can believe it. Buddy and Clipper's pro careers might have been ruined if they hadn't been highly skilled athletes.

The incident suggests to me that there's a fine line between what constitutes a gang and what constitutes a rape.

IT WAS STRICTLY an accident when the best defensive end we've had was involved in an incident that provided the administration with a "last straw" in their effort to fire me.

Boyd Crocker came from a family of firemen and intended to become a fireman himself when his football days were over. He'd hang around the fire stations in his spare time. Go out on calls with the crew. I was happy Boyd had a hobby outside of football.

I take his word there was no way he could have known it was the chancellor's home that caught fire that night. He didn't even know we had a chancellor, as far as that goes. Or that the woman who ran out of the house with the goldfish bowl in her arms was the chancellor's wife.

I'll always believe Boyd told the truth when he said he was sure her nightgown had caught fire when he squirted her with the hose that knocked her backwards into the hedge, broke the bowl in her arms, and killed Travis, her pet goldfish.

Thanks for listening. I might be the only football coach you'll ever know who got fired for becoming an accessary to the murder of a stupid goldfish.

When the Furniture Talked

A DISCUSSION used to come up among us scribes who were raised on radio as to which broadcaster deserved credit for inventing the lateral in the middle of a play that was unfolding before his very eyes in a football game.

There were four likely candidates—Clem McCarthy, Ted Husing, Harry Wismer, and Bill Stern. Any of them were capable, and each of them may have done it at one time or another when no one noticed.

This was radio. Who knew?

Throughout the thirties and forties, which was before the radio had a picture in it, each of those gentlemen possessed a delivery that was easy to identify, and each one achieved a celebrity status to rival that of a movie star.

As a kid who never missed the broadcast of a big sports event on the air, I grew up feeling I knew them as well as I knew Amos and Andy in the evenings or Vic and Sade in the afternoons.

Clem McCarthy turned every event into heavy drama. He had a knack for transforming a boring event into one of life's great occurrences. Somebody wrote that you could only duplicate Clem's voice if you rubbed two pieces of sandpaper together.

McCarthy's trademark opening was, "*Good afternoon, r-r-r-racing fans.*"

In his gravelly voice it was unmistakably Clem McCarthy when you heard: " . . . a left to the jaw by Louis, a right by Louis, another hard right by Louis. . . . and Baer is down . . . five, six, seven . . . Baer is on one knee . . . nine . . . ten! It's over! And the r-r-r-rapid fists of Joe Louis have done it again."

He mostly called horse races and prizefights, so it's not likely that he covered enough football games to invent a lateral.

IF THERE WAS one broadcaster who seriously considered himself on the same celebrity level as, say, Clark Gable, it was Ted Husing. Those who knew him said he worked as hard at his fame as he did at his craft.

Husing was known as a snappy dresser who enjoyed having an attractive lady on his arm. It was further said that the place to look for him in the evenings was at the bar in "21" where he only lifted cocktails with those he considered his equals. Damon Runyon, Walter Winchell, Westbrook Pegler, that bunch.

Husing's style was distinctive. He spoke sharply with jarring pauses for effect. He covered every important sports event from college football to track and field to regattas, always demanding the best positions at whatever event was lucky enough to have him on the scene.

A typical Husing opening:

"Hello, everyone! I'm sitting high atop Michigan Stadium in Ann Arbor where the Wolverines of Tom Harmon, Old 98, will be taking on the indomitable Ohio State Buckeyes today. Welcome to college football on a leaf-turning, windswept Saturday afternoon!"

His peers said that if Husing had seen fit to invent a lateral during the call of a football game, and it had been noticed, he would have justified it indignantly, explaining that the lateral was what *should* have happened.

HARRY WISMER was a football enthusiast more than anything else. He lucked into broadcasting the Detroit Lions games in 1934 when the Lions were new to the NFL. This led to his becoming a popular play-by-play man on college games, but he ultimately returned to the pros as the voice of the Washington Redskins.

Wismer may well have created a handful of laterals in his day. It could have started in his first broadcast of a Redskins game, which happened to be the NFL championship game of 1940 in which the Chicago Bears notoriously thrashed the Redskins by seventy-three to nothing.

Seemingly everybody on the Chicago roster romped to a touchdown that day, and the scoring took place with such haste through four quarters, it wouldn't have mattered if Wismer had invented a lateral from Bill Osmanski to George McAfee, or from Sid Luckman to Ray Nolting, or someone on the bench.

But there are those who say Harry wouldn't have found time to invent a lateral—he was always too busy pointing out celebrities in the stadium who weren't actually present.

"Great to see Gary Cooper sitting there on the fifty with Postmaster General Jim Farley. Coop's a real sports fan. . . . And there's Loretta Young!"

ACCORDING TO EVERY available source, the man who *did* invent the on-air lateral was Bill Stern, the Colgate shave-cream man.

You have to understand that ignoring facts was among Stern's strongest traits. He proved it regularly on his popular radio show, *The Colgate Sports Newsreel.*

As a devoted listener to the program during the war years, I am able to concoct an example that describes the show. Listen now to Stern's voice backed by organ music:

"Reel One. It's Army against Navy in the biggest game of the year. Down there on the field is Army's gutsy quarterback, a kid who vowed he'd never lose to the Middies. That kid's name—Douglas MacArthur. But on the other side is a fullback who swore he'd never lose to the Cadets. His name—Chester Nimitz.

"The game is tied late in the fourth quarter. That's when a skinny kid came off the Army bench and to throw a key block for Doug. His name—Omar Bradley. But a tough little Middie came off the bench and swore to stop him. That kid's name—'Bull' Halsey.

"Still tied with a minute to go, and what's this? Another skinny kid is coming off the bench to call a special play the Cadets have saved up for this very occasion. He sprints across for the winning touchdown. That skinny kid's name—Dwight Eisenhower!

"But that's not the end of the story. Sitting in the Polo Grounds are two visitors from Europe watching their first American football game. Their names wouldn't have meant much to the boys on the field that day, but they do now. Those men were Gerd von Rundstedt and Erwin Rommel, two future German Field Marshals. That's the three-oh mark for tonight."

Sportswriters in Stern's day swear that he came up with more than one lateral on the air.

The first occurred in the 1941 Notre Dame-Navy game when he became mixed up as to whether the Irish's Steve Juzwik or Dippy Evans had the ball. He called it Evans but it was Juzwik who scored, so Bill created the lateral when he realized it.

Another time came in an Army game during the Glenn Davis-Doc Blanchard years. Stern dreamed up a lateral from Davis to Blanchard that resulted in Doc scoring a touchdown, which was fine except that the ball had been in Blanchard's arms the whole time.

Which brings me back to Clem McCarthy and his legendary exchange with Stern after he, McCarthy, had made the greatest mistake of his career. It was the day he called Jet Pilot the winner of the 1947 Preakness Stakes when it was another thoroughbred, Faultless, that won the race.

Jet Pilot had taken the Kentucky Derby two weeks earlier and was thought to be a Triple Crown contender, and Jet Pilot was indeed leading the Preakness into the far turn. But for a matter of seconds, McCarthy's view was obscured by the crowd, and he didn't know that Faultless had overtaken Jet Pilot. On top of that, both jockeys were wearing red silks, which added to the confusion.

As the horses headed into the stretch, McCarthy was saying, "On Trust is still there, but Jet Pilot's got him. It's Jet Pilot by a neck . . . Jet Pilot by half a length . . . It's Jet Pilot by a full length . . . On Trust will be second, and . . ."

Sudden silence on the air.

Then McCarthy said, "Ladies and gentlemen, I have made a horrible mistake. Faultless is the winner. Babe Ruth struck out today. I did the same. I'm in distinguished company."

It has become lore that a week or so later Bill Stern ran into McCarthy at a sports luncheon in Manhattan and teased him about the Preakness call, and insisted that Clem shouldn't have apologized on the air.

And McCarthy replied, "Well, Bill, you can't lateral a horse."

Boyhood Heroes

COUNT ME among those who dabble in college football trivia, which, I've learned the hard way, is better than dabbling in college football parlays.

That said, it pleasures me to discuss a trivia jewel I dug up a while back, one that brought a tender smile to my face. It involves two of my boyhood heroes who constantly hurled touchdown passes of every known variety—bomb, bullet, shovel, fade—and did it for my dear old alma mater.

Dear old alma maters are particularly dear when the football team wins a bunch of games for you.

Slingin' Sam Baugh and Davey "Slingshot" O'Brien were the guys who did it for TCU in my growing-up years.

The trivia jewel: What Sam and Davey accomplished in the seasons of 1935 and 1938 marked the first time in modern college football history that two quarterbacks followed each other back-to-back at the same university and made first-team All-America while leading their teams to national championships. A Double Double.

The feat has only happened on three other occasions since.

Doug Kenna and Arnold Tucker did it for Army with the Glenn Davis-Doc Blanchard teams of '44, '45, and '46. Next was Maryland in '51 and '53, when Bernie Faloney followed Jack Scarbath at the controls. The most recent is USC in 2002, '03, and '04 behind the passing arms of Carson Palmer and Matt Leinart.

Sam Baugh, the rangy six-foot-two, 180-pound "Sweetwater Six-Shooter," did it in his junior season of '35. He led the nation in passing and punting, and with help primarily from a multi-talented halfback, Jimmy Lawrence, Baugh guided TCU to an 11–1 regular season and a victory in the Sugar Bowl over a powerful LSU team that came into the game with a 9–1 record.

TCU's one loss was the 20–14 heartbreaker to SMU in the Game of the Year, a battle on November 30 for the Rose Bowl bid. It brought to Fort Worth the country's best-known sportswriters and sportscasters. College football historians still rank the game among the ten greatest of all time.

That day about forty thousand fans crammed into a TCU stadium that held only thirty thousand. Temporary bleaches were erected in both end zones, and an auxiliary press box was built on top of the east-side stands. Here were two loaded teams with 10–0 season records punching and counter-punching each other throughout the afternoon, and they were tied 14–14 with only seven minutes to play.

SMU's winning play came on a daring fourth-down gamble. It was a forty-eight-yard pass from Bob Finley out of punt formation to Bobby Wilson, the Mustangs' All-America scatback. Wilson streaked down the sideline to the northeast corner of the field, outleaped two Horned Frogs to make a circus catch at TCU's four-yard line, and whirled himself across the goal.

Baugh still had time to pull it out, and came close. He passed the Frogs to within breathing distance of the SMU goal, but time ran out. Grantland Rice put it this way in the story he wrote from TCU's jam-packed main press box:

"Baugh's passes were eating up ground as the final whistle blew and Mustang supporters were in a panic from his deathly machine-gun fire."

The share of the national championship didn't come to TCU until after the bowl games, which calls for a pause to explain the way of the world then.

Shocking as it may seem to the present generation, there was no Bowl Championship Series then. The AP Poll was yet a year away from starting up, and since the middle twenties fans had accepted as gospel the syndicated arithmetic wizards who decided No. 1.

At the end of the '35 regular season, Minnesota with an 8–0 record received the Boand, Helms, and Litkenhous awards. SMU at 12-0 received the Dickinson and Houlgate awards. Princeton at 9-0 was given the Dunkel award.

But the Williamson Rankings and Maxwell Survey waited until after the bowl games to make their decisions. That's where TCU's win over

LSU in the rain and mud of New Orleans by the baseball score of three to two, coupled with SMU's 7–0 defeat at the hands of underdog Stanford in the Rose Bowl, gave TCU the Williamson and Maxwell crowns.

As for that Sugar Bowl, it was good of Slingin' Sam to save one of his greatest games for LSU. All he did was:

Punt a water-logged ball fourteen times for an average of forty-eight yards, hold the ball for fullback Taldon Manton's winning field goal, intercept three LSU passes, make two touchdown-saving tackles near his own goal, and rip off the game's longest run of forty-four yards right at the end that was stopped near the LSU goal, after which in a display of sportsmanship he allowed time to run out instead of trying to score. And Sam played the whole sixty minutes.

After the bowls, Fort Worth fans relished a headline that said: "Dallas Laughed First, Fort Worth Laughs Last!"

DAVEY O'BRIEN was only five foot seven and 150 pounds, but Coach Dutch Meyer claimed Davey's heart outweighed his body. He possessed a marvelous pitching arm and bounced off tacklers like he was made of rubber when he carried the ball in the broken field. Those abilities went along with his other talents to punt, return punts, placekick, defend, call plays, and inspire with his leadership.

O'Brien as a sophomore had been Baugh's backup in '36. That season Sam again led the nation in passing and punting, was a consensus All-America, and led TCU to a 16–6 win over Marquette in the inaugural Cotton Bowl. Those Frogs, having lost six starters from the '35 national champs, still ended up with a 9–2–2 record and a spot in every math wizard's final Top 10.

Davey took over the quarterback job in '37, and the up-and-down season largely served as a warmup for him to perfect his long ball skills. He led the nation in passing and punt returns, made the Fox Movietone News All-America, and despite a 4–4–2 record the Frogs finished sixteenth in the nation although they suffered two tie games and lost two others by one point each.

But that frustrating year was quickly forgotten in '38 when "the little man with the mighty arm" led TCU to what is considered its greatest season in history.

The Frogs demolished their ten regular season opponents with ease and swept to the national championship as recognized by the major selectors: AP, Williamson, Helms, and others. Davey hurled twenty touchdown passes, three against Pop Warner's Temple Owls in a night game in Philadelphia after a three-day train ride, and three each against Texas A&M, Baylor, and Rice. And one crucial TD pass of fifty yards in the thrilling 15–7 win over Carnegie Tech, "the Beast of the East," in the Sugar Bowl. Most of those were long-range bombs that fell into the arms of his prime targets—ends Don Looney and Durward Horner and halfbacks Earl Clark and Johnny Hall.

O'Brien led the nation in passing and total offense in '38 and became a unanimous All-America—he made twenty-one selections. While he was at it, he collected the Heisman, Maxwell, and Camp awards as Player of the Year.

Not that Davey was without help. Center Ki Aldrich was a consensus All-America, tackle I. B. Hale made a handful of first-team choices, and eight of the eleven starters were named All-Southwest Conference.

Not all those details were known to me at the time. You are hardly a stat person at a young age. I mainly knew that TCU was consistently kicking twat on the football field, which encouraged me to think I was growing up in the football capital of the universe.

Thanks to a sports-loving family that included uncles, aunts, and cousins, I was taken to every home game the Frogs played during those giddy seasons while I was going full speed to outrun adolescence. But I was never a kid in the first place.

I didn't read the comics. I read the sports pages. And other parts of the two newspapers in town if the stories had something to do with disasters, wars, dust storms, tornadoes, or gangsters. If Mickey Mouse caps had been available you still would have found me in a kid-size leather helmet lugging a football as I romped around the yard avoiding imaginary tacklers.

My loving grandmother, known to one and all as Mimmie, who would do whatever it took to encourage my interest in sports, or any other honorable pursuit, made me a white cotton football jersey with Slingin' Sam's purple No. 45 on it, and when the time came made me one with Slingshot Davey's purple No. 8 on it.

Of course I could never have guessed that years later as a young guy working on a daily newspaper I would be fortunate enough to meet, interview, and get to know both Baugh and O'Brien. Even to develop a friendship with Davey.

All I can say about those strokes of luck is to repeat the words of a character in a novel I once perpetrated:

"Life's a funny old dog, ain't she?"

More Aerial Bombardment

IF YOU WANT to know how major college football started on this path of deciding games by scores of 65–48 and 52–35 and so on and so forth, travel with me back to 1934, the year that changed the game. You may renew your lust for Jean Harlow, or wish you could have a martini with the Thin Man, or find yourself singing "I Only Have Eyes for You," but work past all that. Think football.

What happened before the '34 season began was that the rules committee, which consisted of a gross of Fielding H. Yosts, instituted a change that would have a profound effect on the game forever.

They reduced the circumference of the football to make it easier to throw. The ball was basically flattened by one inch.

Although the forward pass was legalized in 1906, most coaches kept ignoring it in favor of the power game, a sluggish attack in which the fullback was repeatedly instructed to run the ball up the tackle's ass.

The first time the forward pass attracted attention as a serious weapon was in 1913, when Notre Dame stunned Army 35–13 at West Point. The guys who did the most stunning were a quarterback named Gus Dorais and an end named Knute Rockne. In that game Dorais completed thirteen of seventeen passes for 243 yards and two touchdowns, most of them to Rockne.

The man who was the most impressed by that performance was Dr. Henry Williams, the Minnesota coach. He immediately formed what became known as "the first great passing combination." In 1915 and 1916, it consisted of Arnold "Pudge" Wyman throwing the football to All-America Bert Baston, the game's first glue-fingered end.

In 1916, when those Gophers mopped up on their first four opponents by a combined score of 236 to 0, they were practically handed the national championship. Dr. Williams was so impressed with his juggernaut, he invited Walter Camp, "the father of American football," to attend the Minnesota-Illinois game. Williams even ordered a special box built for Camp in the stadium.

Unfortunately, what Walter Camp saw that day was a shocking 14–9 win by Illinois, a game known for years afterward as "college football's greatest upset." Ironically, Illinois's winning touchdown came on an intercepted pass. Pudge Wyman sailed a ball so far off-target, it hit Illinois's left end Reynold Kraft in the chest, whereupon the startled Kraft was left with nothing to do but trot fifty-five yards untouched for the decisive touchdown.

That result inspired the slogan: "If you live by the pass, you die by the pass."

Which brings to mind that forty years later, when Darrell Royal was guiding the Texas Longhorns to glory, he said it more entertainingly: "Only three things can happen when you throw a pass, and two of 'em are bad."

The forward pass disappeared after Minnesota suffered that cruel embarrassment, but it returned in 1925 when Michigan's Benny Friedman began tossing touchdown passes to Bennie Oosterbaan. Now *they* were being called "college football's greatest passing combination." Those Wolverines outscored seven of their eight opponents 225 to 0. However, back in their sixth game, Northwestern caught them at Soldier Field in a rainstorm that brought winds of forty miles an hour and a field five inches deep in mud. Passes were useless. It was in those horrid conditions that the Wildcats scored a 3–2 upset.

This should have inspired another saying. If you live by the pass, the weather sometimes doesn't.

But meanwhile on the same afternoon of November 7 in Hanover, New Hampshire, the passing game was on vivid display. Dartmouth at 6–0 was hosting Cornell at 5–0 in one of those Games of the Decade that lured Grantland Rice and Ring Lardner to press boxes.

Cornell Coach Gil Dobie, football's winningest coach then, was a true believer in power and defense. He was eager to teach the Dartmouth Indians a lesson. But a strange thing happened. Cornell's players spent the day looking up at footballs flying over their heads.

Dartmouth's tailback Andy "Swede" Oberlander was busy throwing six touchdown passes and setting up two other touchdowns with his arm, most of them going to the immortal halfback Myles Lane and the star end George Tully.

The stupefying final score was Dartmouth 62, Cornell 13. But the stubborn Gil Dobie strained to have the last word.

"We won the game 13–0," Dobie said. "Passing is not football."

ALL OF WHICH HELPED lead up to the downsizing of the football in '34. The skies were suddenly lit up everywhere by the flattened pigskin.

Sam Baugh and Davey O'Brien were only two of the beneficiaries.

The first flinger to take advantage of the rule was Alabama's Millard "Dixie" Howell, "the Hartford Howitzer." In the very season of '34, Dixie led the Tide to an unbeaten season and a Rose Bowl win, mostly by sailing the ball into the arms of Don Hutson, who would become the game's greatest pass receiver.

The Howell-to-Hutson combo not only helped popularize the passing game, it had a considerable effect on sportswriters.

Slingin' Sam and Slingshot Davey were joined in the pass-happy Southwest by Baylor's "Bullet Bill" Patterson, the "Hillsboro Home Run Hitter"; Arkansas's Jack Robbins and Dwight Sloan, "the Pitchin' Porkers"; Rice's "Burly Ernie Lain, the Prowlin' Owl"; Marion "Dookie" Pugh at Texas A&M; SMU's "Rockin' Ray" Mallouf; and Hugh "Lone" Wolfe at the University of Texas.

Almost no quarterback was safe from an attack of the nicknames. The thirties also produced Clarence "Ace" Parker at Duke, "Lethal Cecil" Isbell at Purdue, "Churnin' Vern" Huffman at Indiana, Raymond "Buzz" Buivid at Marquette, Clemson's Banks McFadden—"the Bengal Lancer," "Splendid Sid" Luckman at Columbia, Kenny "Kingfish" Washington at UCLA, George "Bad News" Cafego at Tennessee, and Missouri's "Pitchin' Paul" Christman, a.k.a. "the Merry Magician" and/or "Dizzy Dane."

Into the forties it continued. The world met "Fireball Frankie" Sinkwich at Georgia; Notre Dame's Angelo Bertelli, "the Springfield Rifle"; "Automatic Otto" Graham at Northwestern; UCLA's Bob Waterfield, "the Boomin' Bruin"; "Chunkin' Charley" Conerly at Ole Miss; Stanford's Frank ("Lefty") Albert; "Chunkin' Charlie" O'Rourke at Boston College;

Ohio State's Les Horvath, "the Parma Typhoon"; Alabama's "Hurlin' Harry" Gilmer; Oregon's Norm "The Flying Dutchman" Van Brocklin; "Dazzling Doak" Walker at SMU; and Texas's "Sweet Bobby" Layne, "the Blond Bomber."

Today sportswriting has changed, you may have noticed. A celebrated college quarterback who fails to live up to expectations can become a verb.

By failing to be what was expected of him as a pro, he could one day discover that he's been Ryan Leafed, Robert Griffined, or Johnny Manzieled.

Worse, he could heap enough shame and embarrassment on his career—and his sport—to discover himself Kaepernicked.

The Songwriter

YOU MAY have noticed that the millennium brought with it a generation of warped young people who insist that universities adjust everything to their likes, dislikes, and hectic schedule of protests.

Among their demands was that all of the traditional and familiar fight songs be replaced by something that more closely represents their views on politics. Like, for example, "The Internationale." While most parents were appalled by this notion, as a cocktail-hour piano player I saw it as an opportunity to improve my standard of living. It was an open invitation for me to enter the fight song business.

I sold my first number to an Eastern school where the students had shamed the administration into providing campus workshops on free sex, free drugs, and new ways to combat global warming deniers with pepper spray. I gave them this effort:

> *I ain't got none,*
>
> *We can have fun*
>
> *We can get it done*
>
> *If you gimme some.*
>
> *Get me what I need,*
>
> *Show me the weed.*

That one made it onto the Top Ten list of Rap Poetry.

With that initial success behind me, I offered my talent to a group of schools that were particularly known for their rousing fight songs. I appeared before the football coaches at Texas A&M, Notre Dame, Ohio State, and Alabama to see if they were tired of the "Aggie War Hymn," the "Victory March," "Buckeye Battle Cry," and "Yea, Alabama."

In each case I was told that if anyone tried to change their fight song into anything close to rap or hippie-hop, the person would be lashed with a bullwhip until he was standing in a pool of blood. I took that as a no.

That sent me back East where I was hired by a university whose students had burned down two dormitories and the library and declared the entire campus a safe zone from free speech.

I gave them this, hoping to arouse a little nostalgia in some of the kids.

Janis be dead
But she still livin'
Like Jim Morrison
And John Lennon.
Elvis ain't dead
He still clawin'
Tryin' to climb out
That old coffin.
Don't give up,
Life's a kick.
We still got Keith,
Still got Mick.
The Eagles still sell,
Yeah, yeah. yeah!

I was chased off the campus by a snarling mob of students throwing rocks and fire bombs and yelling that they'd never heard of any of those "old people."

This sent me to a place where I knew I would be welcome. The Northern California College of Wine-Tasting & Staring at the Sun.

I remembered a year ago how a gang of students had stolen a city bus and smashed it through a wall of the campus bookstore to protest the store not keeping enough burkas in stock.

I offered this ditty to the student senate after interrupting a session with their "life coach."

We strong and happy,
Stick out our neck.
We the scrappy
Political correct.
March on, multiply.
Do our duty, diversify.
Bring on the hotties,
Let's go, Jihadis!

MIGHT WORK, they said.

The Scout

I DON'T DO MAYBES, I do talent. That's why the guys who coach hoops come to me for a top prospect, the kid who can deal in the paint, work on top of the iron, stuff the groceries. When I can't find a kid in Africa, I go to Australia, Estonia, Croatia, Sweden, Germany, China, Russia. Finland comes up now and then. I've spent more time in the air than the Goodyear blimp.

But I start in Africa. On average the six-feet-eight kid in Zagreb comes six-feet-eleven in Burundi. All I do is find the kids and place 'em. It's the coaches who have to teach 'em how to piss indoors.

Everybody knows me at the Final Four. I go to the parties, hang with the coaches, the media. The Final Four is where I write up orders for the coming season. Everybody needs a giraffe, an intimidator, an aircraft carrier.

Which is not to say I don't get a request for the front court kid who can wham and jam, spread the floor, zip the pass, bury the three.

I go to Italy for this kid. That's where I found Ugo Gozzi. He was eager to come to the States. His dad had told him stories about the men who'd made it a great country—Cookie Lavagetto, Scooter Rizzuto, Poosh 'Em Up Tony Lazzeri, Lucky Luciano, Momo Giancana. Sometimes he got mixed up.

Ugo Gozzi gave St. Anthony U one All-America season before he was whacked coming out of a tavern on Queens Boulevard. The police said the shots were fired by unknown assailants, and that it may have had something to do with a financial misunderstanding.

IF YOU FOLLOW college hoops, forget the All-America teams. Count on me to have an array of franchises ready to go in the first round of the draft. These are the kids who'll dominate the NBA in the future:

Helmut Dorfner, Iowa Institute of Liberal Arts & Grain.

Played one season of college ball. Raised by an elderly aunt and uncle in a small village near Dusseldorf. The aunt was a bookkeeper for the SS, the uncle served in one of Guderian's Panzer units.

But they weren't Nazis. They were government employees. There were no Nazis in their village. The Nazis were over there somewhere. They taught Helmut to play defense. They'd holler "Sieg Heil" and his right arm would go straight up. He's murder on defense.

Kust Thorfelt, Chicago Freeway Construction.

I know. He's twenty-eight and never played college ball. But he was on three Olympic teams for his native Norway. His dad won the Nobel Prize for Thrift. They say he talks to reindeer. So what? You never overlook a kid who's six feet eleven and white.

Galooma Gwanda, Angola School of War Lords.

A lot of places passed on him. But I say if a kid's near seven feet tall, scores fifty-six a game, you let him wear a loincloth and eat plant life. The Knicks like him. They say he'll learn to like cooked food. He's young.

Mohammed Khadr Ahmed El Mesba, Kentucky Mobile Homes JC.

I first knew him as Billy Simpson, a high school kid who stood seven feet one. But he could dunk a block of concrete into a pickup. He was from one of those towns in Tennessee where they sing "Rocky Top" in church. I've tried to take him to dinner in good restaurants, but he says it's too embarrassing. He's so tall the food slides off the fork before he gets it to his mouth. Won't try a spoon. Stubborn kid.

Soo Koo Ching, Ping Po Province of Learning.

I don't need to remind anybody that Manchuria is no country club. Like how many fish bones can you pick out of one salad? But I'd go back if I could find another Soo Koo. At seven feet eight, she's the tallest player I've discovered. She said she didn't know how to shoot a basketball. I told her she don't have to shoot. Just stand under the bucket and wave at the crowd. She'll hit a ball occasionally.

Since the sex-change she's changed her name to Ching ku-Chen. She'll be the tallest player in the NBA. He, I mean. I can't wait to see how she matches up with the other goons in the league. Him, I mean.

The Chancellor Steps In

MY DUTY as chancellor of this university has led me to be a leader in working to improve the image of collegiate sports. That's why I wanted to make sure that we have nothing but scholar-athletes on our basketball team before we send them off to compete for the $800 million in TV money that goes to the winner of the Final Four.

I don't mind admitting I enjoy watching these youngsters perform their incredible feats on the court. While they bear little resemblance to our average student, our coach assures me that each one is capable of quoting the classic poets and eager to discuss advanced calculus and linear algebra.

Recently when there were nasty rumors circulating about our recruiting practices, I went immediately to Coach Eddie Dunn and asked him if we were conducting our affairs in a proper manner.

He said, "I didn't hear that—what did you say?"

That was good enough for me. I reported my finding to the head of the NCAA's infractions committee. Since our university is a big TV draw, they seemed satisfied.

But as it often happens, the trigger-happy media kept looking into the unfounded rumors about us. Embarrassing rumors that I personally believe were circulated by members of our conference that haven't won a championship in anything since Magellan sailed.

This prompted me to seek out members of our starting five to hear their thoughts on the situation.

I STARTED with Marcus Randall, our big man in the middle, a seven-foot center who carries a 3.6 grade average in smartphone. According to our coach, Marcus is also studying thermodynamics and organic chemistry.

I made an appointment to meet him at his three-bedroom condo and found him reclining in a chair by the swimming pool.

I said, "I'll make this quick, Marcus. Did you receive improper inducements to attend this university?"

Marcus said, "I ain't induced nobody, man. I don't play sex games. What you talking about?"

"Sorry," I said. "I should have phrased it better. I'll put it this way. Are you happy with your curriculum here?"

He said, "Now you really talking crazy. I don't wear no curriculum."

I moved on to Moonglow Willard, who lived next door to Marcus.

Moonglow is our strong forward who carries a 3.4 in stereo history, a successful program we've patterned after Michigan, Alabama, Kentucky, UCLA, Penn State, Louisville, Florida, and LSU.

"How's school, Moonglow?" I asked.

"School be up on that hill?"

"Yes, it's those buildings by the bell tower."

"I was up there once," he said. "They got some funny shit goin' on."

Next I sought out Dwoan Jackson, our other forward. He's a junior who goes six-feet-eleven and leads the team in rebounds. He carries a 3.8 in human hobbies, a program we've patterned after Florida State, Miami, UNLV, Hawaii, Oklahoma State, USC, and Auburn.

I found him on the terrace of his condo with his wife Anesthesia.

They were relaxing in chairs and playing games on their laptops. It took only one glance to see that Dwoan was mowing down two-headed, lime-green aliens.

"How's it going, Dwoan?" I said.

"*Dwoan?*" Anesthesia giggled, looking up at me. "Who is *Dwoan?*"

"Dwoan Jackson?" I repeated, nodding at her husband.

Her husband stared at me. "My name is *Duane*. It's been in the papers."

"I apologize," I said. "Duane Jackson, it is. I saw it written the other way on your enrollment card."

"I was in a hurry," he said, exterminating five more two-headed, lime-green aliens with his forefinger.

I left, having accumulated the information I needed.

There was no need to bother our other two starters—Draino Jones, the shooting guard, and Sprinkler Wright, the point guard.

Coach Dunn had asked me not to barge in and disturb Draino and

Sprinkler while they were reading Chaucer.

I was satisfied with the information I gathered. I'm convinced that with these fine scholar-athletes in our lineup, and the Christian leadership of Coach Dunn, we have an excellent chance to go all the way in the Final Four.

It's the Clock, Stupid

A STORY circulates that an NBA coach once asked his team to play defense, whereupon he was promptly dribbled, bounce-passed, and crammed through the bucket by one of his players in a flying, floating, Phi Slamma Dijon, reverse dunk-burger.

The first time you see a dunk like that it's a grab-your-jaw-before-it-hits-the-floor thing, but it becomes routine after you've watched sixty-seven of them in one game.

I'm sitting here thinking of all the reasons I should fall in love with pro basketball, as so many of my friends have.

It could be that the game's played indoors, which eliminates weather as a factor. The courts are all the same size. The floors are all hardwood. The buckets are all the same height.

None of these short fences in right field or left field or both. None of these outdoor stadiums with wind tunnels, muddy fields, and lousy end-zone seats. Add to it that there are only ten players on the floor at once, not that you'd care to look at any of them other than the guy with the ball.

And you can *see* them. Their faces, their bodies. They're not covered in helmets, sheets of steel, iron masks, Kevlar, astronaut wear. Hoops has intimacy.

It's the opposite of trying to watch twenty-two heavily padded players on a football field. Or twenty thoroughbreds racing against each other at once. Or bevies of athletes running on a track and jumping, vaulting, and throwing things simultaneously. Or 150 golfers competing on a playground that requires two hundred or more godforsaken acres. What's that all about?

It delights the fan that an NBA season lasts longer than a black bear can sleep. Every team plays half the year, then every team enters the playoffs and competes for the other half of the year.

But the big attraction is the drama that comes with the clock.

NOT LONG AGO I made myself watch a complete NBA game on TV, and by that I mean the last five seconds.

It was a playoff game between the Auto Parts and the Climate Controllers. When I tuned in, the Auto Parts were up by six, and were led by a tall player from Eastern Europe with no vowels in his name. Vzly Mllkwk, it looked like on the graphic.

Watching casually, I made a BLT for dinner and cleaned out two closets. By then there were still four seconds left and the score was tied.

I called a friend on the phone.

"Are you watching this?"

"Watching what?"

"The NBA game. The Parts and the Controllers are tied with four seconds left to play."

"Four seconds? I'm off to a dinner party, but I'll switch it on when I come home."

A player for the Parts went up for a soaring dunk. He stayed in the air through a ten-minute commercial break.

Two time-outs were called before he came down.

I'm not sure he came down.

Now an excited announcer told me there were still 1.5 seconds left. Plenty of time for the Parts to score two buckets and send the game into overtime—if they use the clock skillfully.

The phone rang. My friend was back from the dinner party.

"What's the score now?" he asked.

"The Parts need a basket with one point five seconds left."

He said. "I'll make a pot of coffee and settle in to watch it."

Three more time-outs were called by TV during which the Controllers scored a free throw. Which meant that the Parts needed a three-point shot to win if their guy could hit it from out in the hall by the table where you buy replica jerseys.

Now things got iffy. The buzzer sounded as the Parts threw the ball in, but the Parts hurriedly called another time-out. After the TV commercial, the buzzer resumed and the question on everyone's mind was whether the Parts could hit the three before the buzzer stopped.

The Parts hit the three, but the Controllers somehow managed to fire off two shots at the other end of the court before the buzzer stopped buzzing.

Fortunately for the Parts, the shots were batted away by Vzly Mllkwk. He had been put back in the game for that purpose.

I didn't click away until the attractive sideline reporter tried to interview the defensive specialist.

She chirped to Vzly Mllkwk, "What does it mean to you that you were able to save this game for your team?"

"Ya nyeh zna dotsk," he replied.

She turned to the camera, horror-stricken, speechless, and if I had to make a prediction, soon to be unemployed.

A perfect ending to an NBA thriller.

The National Pastime

BASEBALL is a game that was played by Ty Cobb and Babe Ruth, by Joe DiMaggio and Ted Williams, by Mickey Mantle and Willie Mays, and every one hundred years or so by the Chicago Cubs.

But all along, on standby, there's the poetry that certain baseball writers discover about our national pastime.

The poetry results when the baseball writer transforms himself from a seamhead into a member of the literati. He will stop writing his tough, hard-hitting ledes—"Chico likes to throw at white guys, his father mowed their lawns"—and lapse into describing a win streak as something ephemeral and a slump as a catharsis. His byline should read Ralph Waldo Spellcheck.

But I look forward to the transformation. As a baseball fan since I was a lad and the St. Louis Cardinals wore my favorite uniforms, I like to be reminded that the diamond is an emerald chessboard, the ball is a diabolical white speck, and what the pitcher delivers can be a handful of physics, a geometric force.

I likewise enjoy reading about the unwound tensions and eloquent silences that accompany the swat of a long fly, one that slowly but inevitably clears the fence for a homer and is set upon by swarms of ardent fans who have filled the bleachers to recapture the tranquil, rustic tempo of an earlier time in their lives.

This speaks in opposition to the heathens in my circle who write off the sport as watching grown men stand around, spit, and tug at their privates.

I'm obliged to remind them that they must have missed out on the teachings and influences of (1) their daddies, and (2) university professors.

It was the daddies who put the first ball, bat, and glove in our hands. The daddies hit pop-ups to us in the early evenings of those lazy summers.

It was fun, even as we backtracked into thorn bushes, or trotted into the street, eyes upward, and were almost run over by cars. The pleasures would extend beyond time for supper, which compelled various mothers in the neighborhood to do their impressions of Joan Crawford on Benzedrine.

Many of us remember how it was always daddy who hit. A daddy only chased a ball into the street if he wanted to take a closer look at Dorothy Faye Ellis, the divorcee across the street wearing a bikini as she watered the lawn.

As for the professors, they exerted an enormous influence on students who wanted to become sportswriters or maybe take a stab at a novel. The professors convinced them that they could only write a "literary" sports novel if the subject was baseball. It's the only sport professors understand. They understand it because, like cellists, even they played sandlot ball at some point in their youth.

I have a hunch that professors also like the game of baseball because they savor the endless pauses. It gives them time to dwell on the pathos and humor in Milan Kundera.

TODAY I WATCH BASEBALL on TV. You can't go to a major league ballpark now, even if somebody offers you a free ticket. It costs $100 to park, and then you have to walk three miles to the stadium.

Who are these strange expansion teams anyhow? Mariners, Marlins, Devil Rays, Diamondbacks. Wouldn't they be happier at Sea World?

I say bring back the St. Louis Browns, Boston Braves, Philadelphia Athletics, Brooklyn Dodgers, New York Giants, and Washington Senators.

Rebuild Ebbets Field in Brooklyn and the Polo Grounds in the Bronx. Keep the West Coast involved by adding the Hollywood Stars and San Francisco Seals to the league. And with the Washington Senators on hand instead of the Washington Nationals, it's a plus that they won't be wearing the same logo as Walgreens.

I LIKE RELAXING at home and watching baseball on TV. I can have my soft drink and snacks while I wait patiently for that moment when a hitter digs in as the ballpark turns black as the night from pole to pole, and the batter feels the fog in his throat, the mist in his face.

I anticipate the moment when the bases are loaded and the batsman, with an inexplicable response of eye and body, pounds the pitcher's fiendish pellet and relaunches it into an unoccupied region of the verdant outfield for a triple.

With that demonstrative blow, the hitter is forgiven for his unpardonable sins of the past, which was striking out too often in the clutch. Arriving at third base, the hitter straightens his cap and watches the flickering light of ephemeral become a jubilant glow, knowing he was able to outlast the interminable catharsis.

And up in the press box Ralph Waldo Spellcheck hurries to finish his piece in order to rush home, switch on C-SPAN, and catch a little book talk.

Man of the House

IN THE SHOW I'm known as "Big Boo, That's Who." Me, Boo Childers, at your service. If you ain't heard of me, you must have been living in Costa Ricardo or somewhere. Me and my deadly fastball comes with my competitive spirit and killer instinct. It's an institution in the minds of knowledge-type baseball fans.

I'm here to clear up some things with you people before I hurl the opener in the World Series Wednesday night, but I won't be taking no questions.

Too many of you wrote dumb stuff about me and my troubles with Yvonne, my first wife. But I have forgave Yvonne because she helped me develop my want-to when I'm on the hill. She kept complaining about a pitcher with the Reds who become a free agent and was raking in more coin than me.

Me and her did get into a "wrestling-type altercation," as the papers called it, and I got so hot for a minute I did knock her through the screened-in porch of our house in Boca.

She wasn't hurt and nothing come of it but your exaggerated headlines. My lawyer Barry Stamps proved I didn't hit her with a "closed fist," like some of you wrote.

My second wife Maureen was responsible for me finding ways to protect and defend myself. One Saturday morning while I was relaxing and wondering why a guy like me who'd won eighteen and only lost eleven and carried an ERA of 2.56 wasn't worth more money, she asked me to go to the hardware store.

"I'm busy," I said.

"Doing what?" she said.

"Reading," I said.

She said, "So why are you holding the magazine upside down?"

Well, I didn't have to take that kind of nitpicking criticism from nobody.

I slapped her around and shoved her down the basement stairs.

They charged me with one misdemeanor count of "spousal battery." That was funny. The only spousal I've seen was what the plumber replaced on our dishwasher. Barry got me off with a $1,000 fine and a free autograph for the judge's kid. We better-dealed 'em. I paid the damn plumber more than that.

Maureen is who made me decide to give up on marriage. Leave it to ordinary people.

Reba was my first live-in. She was a honey, but that didn't compensate for her being out for whatever she could get out of me. For one thing, she kept bringing up Clayton Kershaw and Cy Young to me. I was familiar with Clayton, but that other guy, I don't know.

She started a phony argument one night and run across the street to a neighbor's house. She called the police and told reporters that Boo Childers had hit her a dozen times with "closed fists," which ought to be worth a stack of Grovers. She knew my arbitration hearing was coming up and it was gonna result in a salary boost that would hover in the millions.

Barry talked her down to $1 mil and three World Series tickets. One each for the handyman, carpet salesman, and insurance thief she was overly friendly with in my estimation and unknown to my knowledge of things.

Angel, my next live-in, come with all the equipment, but she easily qualified as white trash. I should have knowed it. Early in our relatedship she throwed drinks in the face of my skipper and owner when we was having dinner at a strip club on the south side of town. She accused them of sexual embarrassment.

My skipper suggested I take her outside and make her try to catch my 102-mile an hour fastball with her teeth.

He was joking, I thought.

But a week later I come home one afternoon from a matinee with Nanette and I seen Angel and her luggage getting carried off by two guys wearing Halloween masks that made 'em look like that woman politician who's been runnin' for president since the Civil War.

Nanette and me got off to a rough start as soon as we hooked up, but we developed a better relationship when I learned how to spell her name right. I still think it makes more sense with two n's and one t, but what do I know, I've only made the All-Star Game six times.

We've had good and bad weeks outside the bedroom. Currently we happen to be in a bad week. She went on a house-cleaning binge and threw away my priceless collection of comic books and all my GI Joes and Major Matt Masons.

It was like my whole youth didn't mean dook to her. That was a kick to the vitals of my mind, what with me trying to wrap my head around the Fall Classic.

Frankly, I don't know how much more of this kind of abuse I can take around my own home.

A Mortal Lock and
the Hungarian Grip

THE WORLD was closing in on me. The rumors, the allegations, the unsubstantiated reports about my gambling. They were affecting my decisions as a first baseman and causing trouble at home. One jerk even wrote I was a sorry enough person to make a bet with my wife on two bugs crawling up a wall.

That's a sportswriter for you. A guy who'd write something like that about a fellow human. It's why I called the press conference.

"Nobody don't know nothin'," I said to start off. "If somebody knew something, they'd know it and there wouldn't be no talk about it, except between other people in this or that place."

I reminded the reporters that over the last six months I'd read where I had a long history of betting on sports and other things, including baseball, the game I play and hold in reference. Nobody says that about me, Gilly Fowler. Not and walk away unanswered.

A guy stood up.

"Do you deny that you gamble, Gilly?"

I said, "No, I don't deny it. You gamble when you walk out the door of your house. A moron in a car or a terrorist with a sword could come at you from out of nowhere, except you'd have to be somewhere."

"What about sports?"

I said, "You tryin' to win a Puseller Prize or something? Don't you realize if enough people say I bet on baseball, I could be suspended for a year? And if enough people say I bet against my own team I could be suspended for life?"

He said, "We just want you to clear things up, Gilly."

"See, this is serious," I said. "You don't take baseball away from a guy because somebody says this or that. You could say somebody else did something, and what would that prove? You see things in the paper and you wonder why anybody calls it news. News ought to be who won the game, not who did something else. It makes me wonder about the Constitution."

Another reporter stood up.

"All we want to do is put the rumors to rest. It will be for your own good. So you *do* admit you like to gamble?"

I said, "As I have said before, gambling is one of my pleasures. Like some people fish. You could say fishing ought to be against the law, if you think about it. Fish don't ask for that kind of trouble in their lives. They got all they can handle trying to breathe underwater."

The reporter said, "I have it from a good source that a bookmaker in town told the district attorney you lost $45,000 on an oil spill in Alaska. Is that true?"

I shrugged. "I took the Under, so what? I think any reasonable person would have thought ninety square miles was enough."

The reporter said, "It's no secret you go to the race track, right?"

"I go to the track occasionally."

"Weren't you at the track last month when that horse dropped dead in the back stretch? Collapsed and died?"

"I was there."

"We hear there was a disturbance in the Jockey Club when it happened. Furniture was broken. People were punched. Were you part of that?"

"I was in the room."

"It's rumored you had a sizable bet on that race. Is that true?"

"I had the horse."

"You had the horse that *died?*"

"I did."

"How'd you have him?"

"To live."

I pointed to a guy in the back of the room.

He said, "Gilly, do you know a man known as Johnny the Stroller?"

I said, "He's a friend in Texas. Thanks for reminding me of the biggest mistake I've ever made."

The reporter said, "He claims he has three of your World Series rings. Is that so? You admit it?"

I said, "I was short on cash. I paid him off the sixty grand with the rings. It's the only time I've booked a bet myself. So much for being a friendly businessman."

"We'd like to hear about it in more detail, if you don't mind."

I said, "It was a year ago. I was on injured reserve, back in Texas on my ranch. A guy hit a dribbler and slid into first base. Sprained my ankle. Who slides into first base? Jesus."

"It's the bet we're interested in."

I said, "Okay, it's Labor Day weekend. Johnny calls me and says the Texas Department of Public Safety has set the estimated highway death toll at thirty-four. They do this on holiday weekends as a warning to motorists. Johnny wanted the Over, but he couldn't find a book to take anything. Every bookie knew it was raining in South Texas. The roads were slick. Accidents could happen. Would I take it?"

A reporter said, "You bet on people dying?"

I said, "People die all the time. Should they die in vain? Johnny wanted sixty big on the Over. I took it. School was out. No school bus was gonna roll over on me. It was a mortal lock. I had the Hungarian grip on his bonafides."

"But you lost," somebody said.

I said, "You want to talk about unlucky? On a holiday weekend the Texas Department of Public Safety counts the death toll from six o'clock Friday night till midnight Monday. By Sunday morning I'm laughing. I'm winning easy. It's ice cream."

"What happened?" a guy asked.

"I'll tell you what happened. Around noon on Sunday I hear on the radio that eighteen people were killed when a drunk crashed his truck into traffic outside Austin and every vehicle caught fire. This put the death count at thirty-three and I'm sitting on thirty-four. That's when I knew I was beat."

"How'd you know you were beat?" a guy asked.

I said, "*How did I know?* They teach dumbass where you went to school? I knew I was beat because there were still thirty-six more hours for people to get killed and I only had one to give."

His Moment in History

FOR THE FIRST TIME in my life I've wrote a Letter to the Editor of my hometown newspaper, and it wasn't about wars or politics or TV or anything else that makes my ass hurt. The letter was about something important. Major League Baseball and my rightful place in the vernacularism of it.

I'm Smoky Joe Closer. Most baseball fans should remember me from the days when relief pitchers were called relievers, stoppers, and firemen. My name changed that, but I've never got the credit for it from the knuckleheads who cover baseball.

When I was with the Rangers in the eighties we didn't win enough games to be a threat to the standings, but I'd come in and save us our share of games in the ninth inning with my sidearm fastball, which I delivered from a low-to-the-ground, spinning-top type of action, my trademark move.

When I was in my zone I didn't offer up nothing but smoke. It's how I saved twenty-one games one season. It was something to behold, them hitters whiffing at my smoke.

My skipper, One Knee Murphy, deserves a little credit for making me the part of history nobody recognizes. We were holding off the White Sox one night when Murph got the attention of Horse Miller, our pitching coach. He hollered out, "Find me somebody to close this deal, if you're not too busy."

Horse was half-asleep and thought Murph said, "Gimme closer," and he sent me in. Right there is when the reliever, the stopper, and the fireman became the closer.

But my contribution to the great game of baseball and the American way of apple pie was ignored by the knucklehead writers.

That's because they gave the credit to Tony La Russa. Tony was managing Oakland when the As won the '89 World Series. The media decided that Tony invented the word "closer" and hung it on Dennis Eckersley when Eck come in with his slider and sinker and saved thirty-three games that season with an ERA of 1.56. "Closer" stuck to Eck like cheap jewelry on a bimbo.

You can say what I started has turned into a license to steal for today's closers. My pay was lighter than a bag of peanuts, but a guy today whose name you've never heard of pulls down $20 million a season for throwing eight or ten pitches a week at hitters who don't bring enough lumber to lift one over Aunt Edna stooping down to feed her cat.

I don't consider myself in the category with the game's great closers—Eck, Mariano, Goose, Rollie, and maybe others. I just wish I'd been given the fame I rightly deserve.

But like I said in my Letter to the Editor, I'm proud to know in my heart and stomach that I've made a contribution to the game's vernacularism. It permits me to sit here with a peace of my mind in my contentedness and take pleasure in autographing a free baseball for anybody who stops in to make a purchase at Smoky Joe's Tires & Batteries.

That's Smoky Joe's Tires & Batteries. Corner of Old Stove Foundry Road and Crape Myrtle Avenue.

Hurrying Things Up

YOU HEAR it said that baseball is lost on today's youth. It's too slow, too boring. Baseball is not alone in this. Music with a tune has been lost on youth for quite a while. So has dancing, which today looks more like jumping up and down. Also lost on youth are movies in which people talk to each other instead of exploding. But I'm basically here to give baseball a helping hand.

I hope these suggestions will appeal to young people:

It's not a single unless the batter can whip the first baseman in a Taekwondo match.

Brings more physical contact into the game.

Do away with one outfielder.

This will increase scoring and at the same time eliminate so many easy outs.

No more relief pitchers.

The pitcher who starts the game must finish the game regardless of the score, unless he is hit in the face with a line drive more than once. If he's any kind of pitcher, he should be able to finish a game like Red Ruffing, Carl Hubbell, and Robin Roberts used to.

Three strikes are not out if:

The hitter is someone you've heard of, a hometown favorite, or a person with a chance to win the game, provided he's not threatening to break a record held by Joe DiMaggio.

Double plays are left to the discretion of the press box.

A double play may not count if it brings an abrupt halt to a crowd-pleasing rally and is carried by a two-thirds vote of the baseball writers.

Outlaw extra-inning games.

Nine innings are already three too many. In case of a tie score after nine innings, stage a footrace around the bases or a homerun derby.

No consultations on the mound.

The pitcher must not be addressed by a manager, coach, catcher, or infielder during the game. It's time-consuming, and they never discuss anything involving the game anyhow. It's more on the order of, "How was that redhead who hit on you last night?"

"Kill the umpire!"

Make this more than a threat. An umpire may be killed in whatever manner seems fit by the players or fans whenever the replay proves the umpire not only wrong but a complete imbecile.

No more batting helmets.

Put fear back in the game.

No more batting gloves.

If Ted Williams didn't need them, why do you?

Outlaw the bunt.

It only confuses casual fans, rarely produces a score, and most often accomplishes a needless out.

No more celebrities throwing out the first pitch.

It's embarrassing. Too often it reveals their true gender.

Stolen bases.

No base can be stolen unless the bag is actually picked up and loaded into a vehicle and taken to a pawnshop and the receipt is returned to an umpire.

Change the name of the World Series.

It should be known as the United States Series anyhow. Outside of Japan, Cuba, the Dominican Republic, and Puerto Rico, the world doesn't give a hoot about it.

Do away with the first-base pickoff try.

Want to talk about time-consuming? Nobody ever gets picked off. Maybe once every five or six years.

Rethink scheduling.

All games in the regular season, the playoffs, and the United States Series must be completed before the first big college football weekend in September.

No more organ music.

This might be the most important suggestion of all. Institute and promote Organ Night at the ballpark. Here would be an evening at which fans will be encouraged to haul organs from home, church, or a music store, stack them up in a pile in the infield, and have a gala bonfire after the game.

Look, No Hands!

HISTORY HAS IT that the sport of soccer was invented in England in the eleventh century as a game called Kicking the Dane's Head. The Dane has never been identified by name, nor is it known whether he donated his head to the sport before or after he was done in by a poleaxe or a crossbow.

What we do know is that soccer is responsible for more fatalities than any other sport, especially among the passionate fans in Latin America. Down there, soccer riots and the sport's poorly constructed stadiums have knocked off more people than all those who've perished from terrorist activities, military coups, border skirmishes, drug wars, guerilla attacks, voodoo doctors, and suicides inspired by the musical *Evita*.

This is of interest when you consider that a growing number of mothers in the United States are trying to guide their sons toward soccer instead of football in the belief that soccer is a safer game to play.

Soccer is safer in America in one sense. Our fans are seldom known to kill each other at sports events. The American fan deals with a loss by punching a fist through a wall or diving headfirst into a vat of whiskey.

Mothers in the US might change their minds if they'd read the sports sections of the newspapers with more care. They might find an eye-opening story tucked away in a corner of an inside page.

The story would concern the riot at a soccer match in Montevideo that killed 118 fans and injured hundreds of others. The riot apparently started when a visitor was drawn into an argument with a fan of the home club on why bacon is added to a *chivito*, the national sandwich of Uruguay, when it already includes steak, ham, and cheese. Or, an eyewitness said, it could have been something less serious.

WOMEN'S SOCCER is something else. I freely admit I've become a fan of our national women's soccer team. My interest began when they started to win on the world stage. Winning does this. Suddenly we were mopping up on the farm-fed Europeans, the inscrutable Asians, and "the Viking bitches," as they became known to our ladies.

It was great fun to watch the talents exhibited by athletes like Mia Hamm, Julie Foudy, Kristine Lilly, Brandi Chastain, Michelle Akers, Abby Wambach, Alex Morgan, Carli Lloyd, and the others who helped the good old USA win the Olympics four times and the World Championship three times.

It was the squad of Mia, Julie, Michelle, Kristine, and Brandi that did the most for the growth of their sport at home. They did it by winning the 1999 World Championship in the final over China on TV and before ninety thousand in the Rose Bowl. What a moment that was when Brandi Chastain booted the winning goal into the net with her penalty kick. Poor butterflies fluttered in every direction.

These were American athletes who earlier in their careers were dining on 7-Eleven cuisine, staying in "hot pillow" motels, and living on expense money that was less than an IHOP waitress earns in a day—all to promote their sport.

DON'T ASK me why men's soccer inspires unruly activity on the international level, but you can ask me why the men's game will never become hugely popular in the United States until our men win something big.

One. You can't use your hands.

This might be okay for the ladies, but for the American male it's unnatural to play a game with a ball and not use your hands. The fact that men do not use their hands in other activities around the globe is a custom I lay directly at soccer's doorstep. Since our country has become overrun with foreign waiters, this may account for much of the breakage in our restaurants.

Two. The goalkeeper dresses peculiarly.

The goalkeeper wears a different color uniform from his teammates. This is nuts. Why add confusion to an already confusing sport?

I tried to get to the bottom of this one night by discussing it with a waiter I knew in a Manhattan restaurant.

"Humberto," I said, "why does the goalkeeper in the sport you love and care about so deeply dress funny?"

"You must understand soccer," he said.

"I understand soccer," I said. "Brazil wins the World Cup and six hundred people die in the celebration in Rio. But why does the goal-keeper wear green, let's say, when his team is dressed in yellow and blue?"

Humberto said, "The goalkeeper is the only player who can touch the ball with his hands. The referee must be able to recognize the goalkeeper."

I said. "Suppose a team is wearing yellow shirts and blue shorts. Maybe the goalkeeper could wear all yellow or all blue. He would stand out differently, easy for the ref to recognize, but still be wearing a team color."

"Not possible."

"Why not?"

"Because he is the goalkeeper."

I'd never felt so enlightened.

High Sticks
and Body Slams

IF MEMORY SERVES, the teams in the original National Hockey League didn't begin play each year until people were scraping ice off their windshields. And the season seemed to conclude much earlier than it does now, like when every player is partially blinded and in need of surgery on his jaw, nose, and forehead.

Despite my lack of passion for a sport that's played on ice, I could name the original six teams in the league—the New York Rangers, Chicago Blackhawks, Boston Bruins, Detroit Red Wings, Toronto Maple Leafs, and Montreal Canadiens.

The truth is, I only pay attention to ice hockey when the US beats Russia in the Olympics, which is once every century.

My lack of interest has endured through the years even though I allowed a friend to show me the immense pleasure I was missing by taking me to Madison Square Garden one evening to watch a game between the Rangers and another group of athletes from Canada.

This was in the sixties before the league expanded to thirty teams, many of them hilariously located in cities less known for their snowy winters than their traffic. Like Dallas, Los Angeles, and Tampa, to pull three of them out of the penalty box. This, I should add, was in the days before the players were required to wear helmets.

The crowd in the Garden that night consisted of every person who might otherwise be stealing cars, sticking up delis, or racing across rooftops to avoid capture by law enforcement personnel.

When the players came onto the field—ice, rather—I wondered why all of them looked like the Hunchback of Notre Dame.

My friend said it was the nature of the sport. The padding would come in handy because they'd be hitting each other with sticks.

After the teams were well into the contest, a mighty roar occurred.

"What happened?" I asked.

"He lit the lamp."

"He did what?"

"He scored a goal."

"Who did?"

"That guy right there."

"The Quasimodo waving his stick in the air?"

"Yes."

"What was it he did again?"

"He scored a goal."

"How?"

"He slapped the puck into the net."

"What puck?"

THAT WAS precisely when I began to think of ways to make ice hockey more interesting to people like me, who couldn't have told you the difference in a Gordie Howe from a Marceau Philippe de Moose if they took turns pushing me across the blue line, whatever that is.

But before I could give the subject enough thought, I was privileged to see what the crowd liked most about the sport. The gang fights. Not in the stands. Down on the ice.

I was fascinated with the big fight that followed the three little fights. The one where both teams came onto the ice and began punching, slashing, wrestling, hacking, sawing, piling on.

I asked my friend, "What started this?"

He said, "It's the nature of the sport."

"That again, huh?" I said. "Do any of the Quasimodos suffer injuries when they do this?'

"Not that I've ever witnessed or heard about."

MY IDEAS to make the game more appealing would start with the size of the puck. Make it larger, easier to see, to follow. Something roughly the size of a moving van.

I further decided that the league could make do with two teams, the East Coast Mounted Police and the West Coast Park Wardens. The season would then consist of one game.

The puck, or moving van, would be situated in Lincoln, Nebraska, to start. The winner of the Stanley Cup—once it was discovered exactly who Stanley was—would be the team that could successfully shove the moving van into the other team's ocean first.

Those players overtaken by nostalgia could wear ice skates and carry hockey sticks if they wished, but it wouldn't be practical. Might make more sense if they dressed like guys unloading sofas.

We could hear periodic reports from a TV announcer covering the event for whatever national network had lost its mind.

Announcer's voice: "The town you see in the distance is Peoria, Illinois. The people of this community are eagerly awaiting the arrival of an extremely large hockey puck that's expected to arrive here in a matter of hours.

"The Park Wardens have the puck moving in this direction, according to the latest report from our chopper. They opened up a surprise attack on the outskirts of Des Moines when they caught the Mounted Police in a vulnerable tri-state defense.

"Fans of both teams remember too well how the Wardens seized an early advantage in last year's game only to suffer a wrenching loss when they mistook a Mayflower rig for the puck and shoved it into the wrong body of water, having also mistaken Lake Michigan for the Atlantic Ocean."

The announcer turns to a group of the Park Warden fans who have come armed with machine guns and machetes.

"I understand you people are here from Saskatchewan to support your hockey team."

"We're Number One," a fan snarls. "We're goin' all the way!"

"Screw the Mounties," a Park Warden fan yells. "We play Eddie Shore. Old-time hockey."

The announcer says, "That's it from this vantage point. Now back to your regularly scheduled programming."

Tally-ho, M'Lord

AMONG MY FUN-FILLED FANTASIES is the one where I sit astride a gelding and I'm decked out in a red coat, black cap, white jodhpurs, and riding boots. Nearby, a butler stands with a tray to ask if I prefer the Earl Grey or another blend of tea to go with my scones and strawberry jam before the foxhunt begins.

Then comes a follow-up fantasy in which the gelding hurtles me over creeks, hedges, and fences as we keep up with the diligent hounds that are chasing the elusive red fox.

I became intrigued with the sport as a youngster when I gazed at the first oil painting I'd seen of a foxhunt. It was on the wall in the living room of my great aunt's house. It intrigued me more than the landscape of a willow weeping over a stream. The painting of the foxhunt offered flashes of red among the browns, greens, and yellows of the foliage.

Since that time I've seen five thousand paintings of foxhunts. They hang on the walls of English and American castles, stately homes, museums, hotels, restaurants, taverns, and pubs.

Foxhunting was invented by the English in the sixteenth century as a sport for gentlemen and a form of pest control for farmers. Thus it came as no surprise to me that every village in England has a pub called "The Fox and Hounds."

There are almost as many of those in Great Britain as there are pubs named "The Red Lion." Which has nothing to do with lion hunting. The red lion's origin dates back to when the national banner of Scotland was scattered over every kilometer of the British Isles during the reign of King James I, the son of Mary Queen of Scots. He didn't take no from a precinct.

TO BE CLEAR about something. Foxhunting is no sport for softies. A rider has to know how to make a horse do all these equestrian things, at high speed and in a second's notice. Otherwise, the rider winds up in a ditch.

Even the titled English ladies who live in the Downton Abbeys of the countryside learn to ride, hunt, and shoot as young girls. They are also taught to play a musical instrument and recite Byron, Shelley, and Keats before they and their inheritances are sent off to marry the handsome ne'er-do-wells.

You don't want to take a *Vogue* model or a Hollywood actress on a foxhunt with you. All things considered, it's best to bring along a Mitford sister or a facsimile of Lady Mary Crawley.

WHILE FOXHUNTING is centuries old, it's never been a spectator sport. There are simple reasons. Where would you put the grandstands? At the widest creek? The tallest fence? The thickest hedge? There is no finish line, other than where the hounds grow tired, or where the fox dives to safety into his hole, or where the hounds have trapped the pest and turned him into a rag doll.

Only the farmer wants the fox dead. The farmer knows that a fox will eat anything on his property—animals, roots, plants, crops. Not a good thing for the farmer's income.

No person eats a fox, by the way. But the fox will eat a person if he can.

The English country gentleman goes foxhunting with other English country gentlemen and ladies for the thrill of the chase, not the kill. Which is convenient since the clever little fox is almost never caught or killed.

There are no stats in foxhunting—and what is a sport without stats?

There's no National Foxhunting League, no Southeastern Fox Conference, no World Fox Series. And where would the Masters of foxhunting be held? Not at the Augusta National, I'd wager. They don't even allow squirrels.

To bring you up to date, the sport of foxhunting, after four centuries, was declared unlawful in England in 2004. It was the animal rights busybodies who did it. They kept hollering so loudly that everybody in the House of Lords and the House of Commons began to wear earplugs. Various amendments to the law have since permitted hunts to continue in certain enclaves.

I have friends in England who say that given the choice, they would rather go on a hunt for an animal rights activist than a fox.

Not too long ago a story appeared in London's *Daily Telegraph* with a headline proclaiming, "Fox Hunting is the Greatest Sport on God's Green Earth."

This was an aroused support of the sport aimed directly at the activists, not a response to these long-ago words of Oscar Wilde:

"The English country gentleman galloping his horse after a fox is the unspeakable in full pursuit of the uneatable."

I know this. If it weren't for foxhunting, no brave young Englishman would have been able to shout, "Tally-ho, lads," as he banked his Spitfire into a swarm of Messerschmitt 109s in the skies over Kent during the Battle of Britain.

PART TWO
INDIVIDUAL GAMES

Gary Player: "Mr. Hogan, how can I improve
   my game?"
Ben Hogan: "How much do you practice?"
Gary Player: "Around six hours a day."
Ben Hogan: "Double it."

The Tour Stop

GOLF WAS RELATIVELY NEW to me, so you can imagine how excited I was when the PGA Tour came to Knoll Hill Country Club, my home course. It had been coming here for years, but I never paid it much mind, caught up as I've been with trying to keep my car dealership afloat. Not everybody wants a Ford Fiesta.

Anyhow, I was eager to go out on the course and watch Rory and Jordan and Jason and Dustin and other stars of the game. Maybe check out what was new in slacks and slipover shirts. I raced straight to the club for Thursday's first round.

My first shock came when I was forced to park at a church five miles away, ride a shuttle bus, and buy a badge just to enter the grounds of my own country club. The badge cost $5,000, but they took a credit card, and thanked me for contributing to a charity to be determined later.

I was shocked again at how the club looked. Large trucks and trailers and circus tents were spread out everywhere. Wives of members I knew were scurrying around, all of them wearing the same hat, blouse, and polka-dot skirt. They were jumping in and out of automobiles, none of which, sad to say, was a Ford Fiesta.

"Hi, Millie," I said to a wife I knew. "Did Fred come out today?"

"Sorry, I'm in a hurry," she panted. "Ted Hatch's wife wants to go to Target and Clay Dugger's wife needs to find a pet groomer for her poodle."

"Wives of pros," another lady in a polka-dot skirt explained. "They keep us hopping. But—you can't run a tournament without us volunteers, can you?"

Millie sped away in a white sedan with a large logo on the door. The logo resembled a yellow layer cake with three golf clubs sticking out of it.

Another shock came when I entered the clubhouse and a security guard pushed me up against a wall. I wanted to go in the locker room. "Players and officials only," the guard said gruffly.

"I'm a member," I said.

"Move along, buddy. The hallway is crowding up."

"This is my club," I said. "I'd like to use a bathroom."

He put his meaty paw on my chest again and shoved me backward as he spoke into a two-way radio.

"Ralph, I've got a Code Four by the locker area. Send somebody down here to help me out with this clown."

His message was clear. I hurried downstairs to the Men's Grill, only to bump into another security guard.

"Wrong badge," he said, blocking the door.

Pointing to the $5,000 badge on my shirt, I said, "This is supposed to be good for the clubhouse."

"You're not a Patron."

"A what?"

"Patrons only. Sorry."

"How do I become a Patron?"

He said, "You buy a Patron's badge for $10,000. If you were a Patron, would you want to let a guy like you in for free? Move along, please."

I hoped to find a bathroom and a snack in the Mixed Foursome Room, but I ran into another security guard. He squeezed my arm until my eyes watered.

I yelled, "What are you doing? I'm not a criminal!"

"You're not a Saint either," the guard said.

"I'm not a *what*?"

"This room is for Saints. You don't have a Saint's badge."

"What does it cost to be a Saint?"

"I hear it's $25,000. But it comes with a reserved seat in the luxury box behind the eighteenth green if you want to watch golf in comfort."

"Is every golf tournament like this?" I asked.

"How the hell would I know? Move it, okay?"

I thought I might find a bathroom and food in the teenage recreation parlor. It used to be called the Peppermint Lounge, but it's been renamed the Rap Trap.

Another security guard was on the door. I peeked around him and saw adults sipping cocktails, filling up plates with food.

"Sponsors and their guests only," the guard said.

"What sponsors?"

"The banks, insurances companies, investment people. You think you can put on a golf tournament without sponsors. Where you been living?"

I GAVE UP on the clubhouse and moved outdoors. After I waited in line for twenty minutes to use a port-o-let, I strolled over to a concession stand.

I stood in another line there for forty minutes to buy a hotdog for $18. But I wanted mustard and sauerkraut on it. That sent the price up to $35.50. They were out of ice, which meant the warm Coke was only $12.

The best spot to watch golf was by the green at No. 9, a friend had said. I managed to push in among the crowd around the green. I caught a glimpse of three golfers down on their hands and knees. I wondered if one of them had lost his contacts.

"Which one is Jordan Spieth?" I asked a fellow next to me.

"He's playing in the Malaysian Open this week."

"Oh? I read in the paper he was here."

"They pay a $13 million appearance fee over there. I can't blame him."

"Who are these three coming up?"

The fan said, "Let's see. That's Rip Claunch behind the tree . . . uh, that's Cusser McAdoo in the bunker . . . and the guy over there waiting on a ruling by the water is Tiny Shacker."

"Those are touring pros?" I said.

"Don't follow the game much, do you?" the guy said. "Rip Claunch won here last year."

I could only say, "Huh."

He said, "Don't look for Jason Day. Jason's taking the week off. Bad back."

I said. "The paper said he was here too. I guess Dustin Johnson is out on the course somewhere."

"Not this week. Dustin's in Buenos Aires. The Argentine Open is paying him a $10 million guarantee, or so I've heard."

I realized I was wasting my time trying to watch golf. I hiked over to the area where I could catch the shuttle back to my car. That's where I found a man squatting on the ground, moaning, holding his head in his hands.

"You don't look well," I said. "Anything I can do?"

"Yes," he said. "You could see that this golf tournament is over with as soon as it's humanly possible."

I said, "You don't like golf?"

He said, "I like golf fine. But the tournament committee has blocked off the street to my house, and I don't have the right badge to get back home."

Pushing the Envelope

IT WAS PLEASING to learn that the golf course design business had made a recovery from the overdevelopment of dreary layouts in a glut of gated communities. The Era of Golf for Geezers had come to an end, thankfully.

My golfing friends told me there were refreshing things happening today. Four dynamic young architects were now in demand and were busy "pushing the envelope" in their trade.

After researching them, I invited the four designers for drinks at the Marriott where I was staying while attending a regular event on the tour that was sponsored by a food chain. It could have been a pill, maybe an ointment.

I first called on Chuck Wade to tell me about his new project. He had worked for Alistair McSwath, the man who designed Cypress Pines.

"Have you been to Little Bighorn?" Chuck asked me.

"You mean like the Battle of Little Bighorn?"

"That's it."

"We stopped there once on a family vacation in Montana."

"Then you saw the tombstones of the Seventh Cavalry inside the little fence? On the hill where General Custer got his?"

I said, "It was amazing to stand there and think about what took place. Custer got hit on all sides by the Sioux, Cheyenne, and Arapaho."

"My eighteenth green sits next to the graves. Clubhouse behind it."

"Your eighteenth green is next to the dead soldiers?"

"Right beside it. My money people made a deal with the Indians. The rest of the course tumbles down the fields to the river. The first tee's not far from the entrance to the casino."

"What's the name of the course?"

"Terrific name. St. Andrews at Custer's Last Stand."

SANDY PRATT had moved dirt for Donald Ritz, the man who designed Oak Canyon. What Sandy had learned about drainage, he said, you couldn't buy.

His latest project was south of the Equator. An island near Antartica. His money people assured him it was the most unique parcel they've acquired.

I said, "Sounds too cold for golf, if you don't mind me saying so."

"Climate control plastic bubbles cover every hole."

"Really? Where in the world will golfers stay when they go there?"

"Igloos."

"Igloos?"

"Don't laugh. Choices will be available. Super luxury, luxury, middle income, public course."

"How do you reach this place? Go to the Falklands and take a left?"

"You could. It's easier to go to Cape Town and take a right. The landing strip will be ready next year."

"How do you get there now?"

"Hovercraft," he said. "There are two a week from Queen Sheila Bay."

I said, "Golf among the icebergs. I can imagine one thing going for it. The course will never be crowded."

"We're dealing with one problem. When it's 100 degrees below zero, you'll have to scoot lively when you go from a green to the next tee. We're experimenting with heated sleds."

"I'd vote yes on those. This is a second-home development?"

"Third home. It's over for the second-home market. You can't get a tee time anywhere. We have a great name for the club."

"What are you calling it?"

"It honors our top investor. St. Andrews at Ice Station Trump."

I TURNED to Troy Wheeler. He had driven a tractor for Pete Fry, the man who designed Lumber Valley on Hilton Head.

"What's up with you, Troy?"

"Things couldn't be better," he said. "I have a piece of the real estate action with my current project."

"Where is it?"

"Sudan."

"Sudan?"

"My money people have never been this pumped up. We first tried to buy a parcel in Chad, but the elephant poachers ran us off."

"I've heard that can happen."

"They did the next best thing. They bought 1,500 acres from a group that inherited the land from the family of Muhammad Ahmad al-Mahdi."

I said, "The al-Mahdi. I've come across that name in reading. Maybe it was a movie. Have you started work on the course?"

"We're still excavating bones."

"Dinosaurs?"

"No. Human."

"Uh-huh."

"More than we expected, to be honest."

"Interesting, Do you have a name for the club?"

"A good one. St. Andrews at the Siege of Khartoum."

I TURNED to Frank Sanders. He had deepened bunkers for Robert Tartan Crane, the man who designed Samovar Hills in a suburb of Moscow . . . where they play the Russian Masters every year.

Frank said, "I'm assuming you've never been to Afghanistan?"

"That is correct," I said. "And with any luck I never shall."

"You'll want to go when I finish my course. It's halfway between Kabul and Bagram Airfield."

"You're building a course in *Afghanistan?*"

"I'm excited. My first hole goes from Motel 6 to the Dollar Store. A par five. The second hole doglegs around Ace Hardware. Par four. Everything is underground. The golf course, everything."

I couldn't fight off a chuckle.

"Laugh if you must, but it's all over for inconvenience. People want to golf where they live. Walk out your front door, take the escalator down, you're on the first tee. Come off eighteen, buy wicker furniture, eat Thai, ride the escalator home. No danger. A Marine battalion is on duty twenty-four hours a day to guard against incursions by the hajis and Ali Babas, as our troops refer to them. It's a win-win proposition."

"Do you have a name for the club yet?"

"We're thinking about St. Andrews at United States Air Forces Central Command."

"It's a grabber," I said, motioning for the check.

Voices of Authority

ONLY MOMENTS AGO, here was Rory McIlroy. Ankle-deep in the cabbage, the wind against him as it howls in off the Atlantic, the bunker-guarded green more than 210 yards away. But watch what happens when Rory's nine-iron meets his rock . . .Yowzer!

Good afternoon, golf fans. I'm Don Void, and what a feast we have for you on the exotic New Jersey shore. The oil slick is under control, the red tide has receded, and we're coming to a climax in the final round of the World Championship Estate Planning Classic presented by the Bank of Kowloon.

Working with me on the eighteenth hole today is my good friend Floppy Clifford, runner-up in the PGA Championship this past August. Floppy will be providing the lighter touch as we move along throughout the action, eh, Floppy?

"I would have won that PGA if God hadn't taken a dislike to me for no reason I can think of. I go to church every Easter."

Right you are, Floppy. While Rory is on the green doing a little housekeeping, and before we go to the final-round fireworks today, let's catch you up on what took place Thursday, Friday, and Saturday here at Five Bluffs Golf and Beach Club, one of the most challenging layouts in these United States.

Tiger Woods had the crowd buzzing early Thursday by making one of his patented comebacks. He fired a five-over seventy-five. Tiger thought his score should have been much lower—he didn't hit a bad shot. But he likes his game and the progress he's making.

Tiger held the lead for six minutes, but that's when the rookies took over. Howell Rake was the first to the cabin with a ten-under sixty-two.

He was later tied by five other players whose names aren't that familiar to me, if you want the truth.

Friday was the day Brad Method made a move. He fired a sixty-one and tied Howell Rake for the thirty-six-hole lead. Here we see Brad launching a 310-yard five-iron onto the par-three ninth. And there's Brad's wife, Denise, showing us two reasons why she was crowned Miss Oklahoma last year, not to speak off-color.

The big news was Tiger making the cut. It leaves him twenty-two shots off the lead, but that's no hill for a climber, right, Floppy?

"Nobody suffered more bad luck than I did in the last round of that PGA. It was bad enough my tee shot on eighteen hit a spectator, but to have it bounce off that woman's skull and wind up with the lie I had in the bunker . . . "

I'm anxious to hear more about it, Floppy, but now I want to remind our viewers that the wind blew seventy miles an hour on Saturday but it didn't stop the birdie parade. Howell Rake and Brad Method remained tied for the lead after they both shot a fifty-nine.

It's sad to report that Tiger stumbled to an eighty-seven, although none of it was his fault. He has a lot of strokes to make up. I'm not sure of the exact number—it's somewhere around forty-five, forty-six. But that's nothing he can't overcome if he gets it going. We have to keep in mind that Tiger Woods is Tiger Woods.

Now to bring in our expert commentators. Julia Ross Fletcher Stevens of LPGA fame is stationed at No. 14. Come in, Julia.

"I have a cold, Don. Can somebody bring me a box of tissues?"

Can you speak up? We can barely hear you, Julia.

"That's because I have a *head cold*! Am I talking to myself or what?"

Say again, Julia?

"Never mind. I'll use my shirttail."

A little trouble with the feed, folks. We'll be going back to Julia. But on to No. 15 and our good friend from over the pond, Peter Brace-Asher. Welcome aboard, Peter.

"I'm afraid you've caught me in the loo, old chap. Be with you in a sec."

Not an unreasonable request, right, Floppy Clifford?

"That lie I had in the sand, I couldn't have got it out in one try if I'd used a post-hole digger. It took three pokes with the wedge. But when I made it to the green, what do I find? My ball is in a spike mark that must have been dug by some animal trying to go to China, and . . . "

"I'm back, chaps. Peter Brace-Asher at your service. Jolly good fun to be here, I must say. What marvelous stuff we're seeing from the boys as they nestle their wedges into the pins on these intoxicating greens. As for the fifteenth, well, what a devilish thing it is. One bloody slip and you're consigned to a watery grave. Not exactly what a fellow has in mind to my way of thinking. Over to sixteen, then."

And the reliable Vern Utterance. Come in, Vern.

"Hi, this is Vern Utterance. I'll be reporting from the six hundred and forty-five yard par-five sixteenth that—no, wait a minute, that's eighteen. Sorry. I've just arrived from the figure skating in Brussels. I see I'm at the five hundred and twenty-three yard par-four sixteenth, and from my vantage point I can see a long stretch of green grass. The grass appears to stretch as far back as the tee. Over to seventeen and my colleague Frank Murk."

"This is Frank Murk at the seventeenth where we've seen thirty-eight pars, two hundred and forty-nine birdies, and sixty-two eagles posted by golfers who range in height from five feet five to six feet two and weigh an average of one hundred and sixty-two pounds. Most of the pros from Texas and California were born there. Back to you, Don."

And just in time to show you the videotape of Rory McIlroy missing that two-foot birdie putt. Man, that could cost him $12 million before this is over. Watch as Rory's ball curls around the edge of the cup, and then how his putter takes a nasty divot out of the bent green—my word, that divot is big as a grapefruit. Now we see the muddy divot hit Jordan Spieth in the chest—splat! But Jordan laughs it off, as all good sportsmen do.

Meanwhile—excuse me, they're talking in my ear.

What? The News Division is doing *what*? You're kidding. No? You're not kidding? You're pre-empting us? You're taking our viewers away from Tiger Woods and *a golf tournament* so you can show a tidal wave in *New Guinea?*

Well, that's it for us, friends. It's not my call. I want everyone to know that. But I'm not signing off until I say that if anybody in our News Division thinks it's more important than golf for our viewers to watch cannibals try to learn how to swim, they can . . .

Trouble at Old Baffy

DEAR BOARD of Governors and Members:

I write to you out of frustration over many of the changes happening to Old Baffy in the name of improvement.

Most of you are aware that my grandfather was a charter member of Old Baffy, my father was president of this club, and I have been both president and chairman of our annual event on the PGA Tour. Speaking of which, let me say that I took a little more pride in our tournament when it was known as the Old Baffy National Invitational. But these days the Hostess Powdered Donut Classic does not roll easily off my tongue.

But on to more important things. Was there a pressing need to chop down the grove of one-hundred-year-old oaks on the right of fairway on No. 1 to relocate the children's playground? To say nothing of the loss of those wonderful trees, wasn't the hole challenging enough without the golfer having to cope with the infuriating squeals from the urchins on their slides and climbers?

For years I thought the playground was well-situated across the street from the private homes on Old Baffy Drive. We watched those homes continually come up for sale when the residents tired of being annoyed by the screeching of the hell-bent holy terrors.

Why did it not occur to anyone on the Board that the constant turn-over of these homes brought in members who paid a greater initiation fee and higher monthly dues, which therefore provided increased revenue for the club?

Whose brilliant idea was the petting zoo halfway between the tee and the green at No. 6? I have nothing against sheep, guinea pigs, goats, llamas, rabbits, and ponies. But they do present a distraction for the golfer. Even more so, I think, than the new bridge over the swamp area. I have two words for the Greens Committee concerning the bridge: hand rails.

I would like to suggest a sign to post at the petting zoo. It might attract the attention of our young mothers since one of them misplaced her child last week for eight hours. The mother was eventually located gambling at mah-jongg in the clubhouse after her round of golf. The sign should say:

A goat is not a babysitter!

WHOSE BRILLIANT IDEA was it to remove the pond and our lovely rippling stream that caused three holes to be shut down for six months? I've heard the suggestion came from a touring pro who said we should do this to make our course a fairer test. What? Shorten it to fifteen holes?

So we rush off to fill in the pond in front of No. 13 and do away with the stream that borders No. 15 and No. 16.

I've been told the touring pro's name is Hook McCall. Who in the world is Hook McCall? He's nowhere to be found in the PGA Tour Players Guide. I would remind the board that when Phil Mickelson suggested we dig up our bent greens and replace them with a more durable surface, it was Phil Mickelson talking.

I might add that it wasn't Phil's fault that the wrong base was used for the new greens causing them to be redone at a ridiculous cost. Only the Board can be blamed for this oversight.

One of these days I'm going to find out who determined that we needed a monkey farm next to the snack shack between No. 11 and No. 12. What exactly is the lure of having monkeys to look at while you're having a beer and a hotdog or hamburger?

Not that our monkeys are monkeys. They're chimpanzees. And chimps are apes. Chimps are smarter than monkeys, and they can be practical jokers. No monkey this past spring would have been smart enough to have wriggled through the wire and stolen Rickie Fowler's ball in the fairway, which cost him a two-stroke penalty in our tournament.

ABOUT REDECORATING the clubhouse. I'm sorry, but Old Baffy doesn't look like the same club to me. A question for the Board. What did you do with all the dark wood and brass?

Second question. How many public restroom floors did you tear up to find enough white tile for the Veranda Dining Room? Am I supposed to go in there to dine or donate blood?

The idea of a large outdoor balcony upstairs off the Mixed Grill with tables and chairs for cocktails was a good one, but I'm certain that with a little more planning the balcony could have been built to provide a view of the golf course rather than the south parking lot.

About the new chef. I have been afraid to try anything on his art-sy-crafty dinner menu, and here's why. A week ago my cheese omelet at breakfast would have known a better life as a mouse pad. His so-called cream gravy turned my biscuit into a piece of French pastry. And I wished that my order of bacon had been, well, let's say, cooked. Instead, it came out imitating a case of trichinosis.

Please accept these comments as well-intentioned. Nobody loves Old Baffy more than I, R. B. ("Rule Book") Stringer.

The Fabric Guy

BILLY DON BLAZE is set decoration. One of the pros that we in the press call part of the fabric of the tour. But he provides a valuable service. The top players need people to beat every week. In Billy Don's twelve years on the scene, he has yet to win a tournament, but he's become a familiar name. Maybe not as familiar as some others, but I'd heard of him and wanted to do a piece on him. Tell the story of a fabric guy.

I caught up with Billy Don on the practice range at Shallow Valley Country Club at one of the two-dozen events on the tour that calls itself a World Championship. I extended my hand, gave him my name, and announced that I was with *Golf Delirium* magazine.

He refused to look at me. Kept hitting balls with his driver that stayed in the air until they disappeared and wouldn't come down until they were somewhere over the Himalayas. Today's equipment continually amazes me.

I smiled at his caddie. The caddie looked away.

I smiled at a man I presumed to be Billy Don's swing coach. He ignored me. Kept reading a book by Werner von Braun.

Billy Don finally acknowledged my presence.

He said, "Do you have an appointment?"

"Well, no, but . . ."

"See, that's the thing," he said, cutting me off. "You must be blind, you don't see that rope you ducked under? You come in here to *my* office and it don't matter I'm working. You media guys."

"But I . . ."

"What if I came in your office when you were working? Walked right in. Didn't call ahead. What would you do?"

"I'm not sure it's the same as . . ."

"I'll make this quick. You want to do an instruction piece on Billy Don Blaze, see my agent."

I said, "My magazine is more interested in a feature of an average guy on the Tour who . . ."

"I'm an average guy, huh?"

"Only in the sense that you've never . . ."

"Let me straighten you out. Winning don't mean squat out here. Ask me if I want to win a tournament or do I want to bank four million a year? What do you pull down? A hundred? Hundred and a half? I make more than that in a week. So who's the smart guy here?"

I said, "I intend to write about the money, but . . ."

"That's not what you'll write. I'll say A, B, C, you'll write D, E, G. I'll say Monday, you'll write Thursday. You writers ought to be like the TV people. They build us up. You tear us down."

I said, "If you'll answer a question about the majors, I'll . . ."

"See, you sneaked in a question, but I'll answer it—you hit a nerve. I'll tell you about a major. A major is just another golf tournament, except they're played on tricked-up courses to make us look like we don't know which end of the club to hold. Ask me if I'd rather win the Tylenol Phoenix or the Masters. I'll take the Tylenol any day."

"What about history? A major has . . ."

He said, "History is for books."

"You don't want to be part of golf history?"

"Yeah, put me in a book. Lot of money in that."

I said, "One or two more questions and . . ."

"I ain't talking about my equipment."

"I wasn't going to ask about that, but why won't you talk about it?"

"Equipment is personal."

"Okay by me. So may I ask if you're still a man of God?"

"God?" he said. "You mean like . . . up there?"

"That would be Him."

Billy Don thought about it and said, "I'd have to say God helped me through my four weeks of college . . . and through two years on the Web. com. But he hasn't helped me so much on the tour."

"Oh? Why not?"

"Like today. On fourteen. I'd like to see God try to hit a five-iron out of that stinking divot he put me in. If he thinks he can play, let him come down here."

Golfer Seeks Cure

THE RECREATIONAL GOLFER is never a completely contented person because, well, because he plays golf.

He's taken lessons from every club pro in town but nothing helps his game. He's been to every golf school and golf academy in the state, but no help there either. It has yet to occur to him that these teachers may not want to help him too much or he'd stop coming back. Bad for business.

He watches every tournament on TV in search of a swing tip. Even the LPGA, even the Seniors. His dream is to break ninety without any mulligans.

He does experience moments of gratification. It's when he manages to make two pars in an eighteen-hole round and hurries home to sit down and tell his dog about it, stroke by stroke, while the faithful border collie listens with fascination.

Meanwhile he remains caught up in the rash of instruction books that are constantly written by experts no one has heard of, including him.

Here are passages from some of the current works on his book stand: *How to Play Your Best Golf with Rich Guys* by Skeet Grinnell.

The Grip: Keep a firm grip on your money clip when golfing, dining, or drinking with a rich guy. This is important with rich guys who have been schooled in the Eastern part of the United States. Most of their slacks don't have pockets.

The Country Club: Check out a social function at any country club before you apply for membership. If you see any pink, lime, or flowered slacks and striped blazers, you may want to reconsider that one.

The Director of Golf: He will be the guy selling you a driver you can't possibly need. You already have fifteen.

No Set of Golf Clubs Has the Slightest Regard for Your Mental Health by Dr. Simon Clagg.

Long Irons: Throw them in the nearest river, lake, ocean, creek, or sewer, depending on the type of layout your home course is built on.

Hybrid: This is a reasonably modern weapon that many think of as a safety valve, a keep-it-in-play club. However, the clubhead on the hybrid seems awfully small to me when you're trying to hit something even smaller.

Short Irons: The shaft on the 7-iron breaks best when slung at a rock fence. The 9-iron can be relied upon to take the deepest divots out of the fairways when a shot goes astray.

Sand Wedge: Touring pros today carry eight in their bag, but you only need one to put a savage dent in the hood of your car after a frustrating round.

The Putter: No golfer can have too many putters. The average country club member owns fifty to seventy-five putters, but I would stay away from those that resemble a tenor saxophone.

What Par Doesn't Know Doesn't Hurt It by Michael Sims.

Do not be intimidated by par. Stand up to par. Simply because par says it is three, four, or five on a hole doesn't make it so. When keeping your score, always factor in what it means to your peace of mind.

Keeping Up with Your Swing by Percy Grinder.

The Swing: Most recreational golfers do not know what they look like when swinging a club, although they've watched videos of themselves in golf schools and academies. The golfer sees what he wants to see.

The golfer may think his swing is starting to look like Jordan Spieth's when it would be more accurate to say it resembles an overweight man trying to revive interest in the hula hoop.

The Stance: To achieve the best results, follow these tips:

Stand erect, but not too erect. Your feet should be wider than your shoulders, but not too wide. Bend over from the waist, but only slightly. Flex the knees, but not too much.

When you feel you are in the proper erect-bent position, have somebody hand you the golf club.

Now, with the club in your hands, and you're using the correct overlapping grip, go over the checkpoints.

Are you too crouched? Are you too erect? Is your weight evenly distributed? Can you lift your right heel without too great an effort? Are you pointed in the direction of the fairway or green, whichever may be the case? Is there nothing else on your mind at the moment? Car payment? Home loan? Electric bill? Divorce lawyer?

When your mind is completely clear, and you are in the ideal erect-bent position, there is one more thing that may be worth considering before you swing the club.

You might want to let those angry groups behind you play through.

The Obscure Slam

SO THIS SPORTSWRITER walks into a press room . . .

That sounds like the start of a joke, right? But it isn't. Actually at this writing it's been my job to spend one year and four months of my life in Augusta, Georgia, covering the Masters for sixty-eight consecutive years.

That's a Masters record for journalists that stretches from the Augusta National veranda to a public course in Istanbul. Each day I go to the mailbox to see if the prize money has arrived yet. No luck so far.

But it's been a great gig.

I started in the old press tent in 1951. It overflowed with grown men in fedoras bumping into each other, or their folding chairs and Smith-Coronas. A few forty-watt bulbs dangled from the ceiling. There was a din of phones ringing and bells pinging on wire machines. The place was dense with cigarette smoke. I knew this was where I belonged.

Western Union operators were clacking on their whining contraptions in a cramped alcove sending out urgent pieces about Ben Hogan and Sam Snead, the only two golfers of interest in those days. Sports editors back in the offices in New York, Chicago, even Fort Worth, took a dim view of their writers filing stories on golfers they'd never heard of.

The tent was open at two ends—we could catch the breezes. Augusta used to offer a buffet of weather in one week—ideal, hot, windy, warm, rainy, freezing.

The writers were still dressing in coats and ties at golf tournaments. I suppose it was because Grantland Rice did. I was excited to see the nattily attired Rice at my first Masters. This saintly gent in a shirt, tie, sweater, checkered jacket, and light gray hat. I saw him across the crowded tent. But I was too shy to introduce myself to the gentleman who, along with bringing dignity to my profession, had given the Masters its name. Three years later he passed away.

In 1953 we scribes were delighted to find that the tent had been re-placed by a Quonset hut. Although it was as poorly lit as the tent, it was larger and roomier. There was more elbow space and aisles in which to move about without knocking a colleague's Pulitzer effort sideways.

I was privileged to meet Bobby Jones back then. He used to invite two or three writers to lunch with him in his cottage most days of Masters Week. I was fortunate to be invited to one session. My relationship with Ben Hogan had something to do with it.

Jones couldn't have been more gracious. Except when I wanted to talk about Bobby Jones, he wanted to talk about Ben Hogan.

Another brush with him came on the Augusta National course before the 1954 Masters began. Writers were welcome to play the courses for free if they showed up on the previous weekend. I was standing on the fifteenth tee with two other writers when a golf cart pulled up behind us. Sitting in the cart were Bobby Jones and Clifford Roberts.

They both smiled at me. Cliff Roberts also associated me with Hogan. He said, "We came out to see how the new mound is playing on this hole. Don't let us bother you."

Bother me? Why would it bother me? I only have to hit a drive with Bobby Jones watching. Happily, my soaring hook didn't hit anything but a pine tree.

Within the Quonset hut there slowly emerged an Interview Area. Daily leaders were brought in, and on Sunday night the losers and the winner appeared. It was standing-room only, and the questions were mostly hollered out by those writers who fancied the sound of their own voices.

I could hardly forget the Wednesday afternoon that Claude Harmon, the 1948 Masters winner, was escorted into the Interview Area. He had remarkably made back-to-back hole-in-ones in the Par-3 Tournament.

In the midst of the interview, a writer from the Midwest (name with-held out of respect for his family) shouted out, "Claude, when was the last time you made back-to-back hole-in-ones?"

Gad, this idiotic question had come from one of our own?

The laughter at the writer's expense was raucous. But before it died down, Bob Drum, my good friend from the *Pittsburgh Press,* standing next to me on the back row, could be heard above it, as he bellowed:

"Where's my hat?"

THE INTERVIEW AREA saved us the trouble of tracking down the competitors elsewhere, but it took away part of the fun in that exercise. The field was smaller and every competitor lockered upstairs in the main clubhouse, which is now exclusively a dining room. Hogan on this side of the room, Snead on that side. Tables, chairs, and sofas in between.

It developed into a competition for those of us on strenuous deadlines. It involved climbing over fellow typists and corners of furniture to obtain a quote from an immortal. Not that I enjoy a scrum. But I was young then.

The Quonset hut expanded to include an upstairs loft for writers as the coverage grew, and an indoor area turned up for the traditional pimento cheese and egg salad sandwiches, two favorites of Chairman Clifford Roberts. I should have bought stock in them. They exist to this day, as much of a Masters fixture as Magnolia Drive.

In the early nineties we arrived to find ourselves in an enormous facility that could pass for a lecture hall. It came with a dining room on the top level above the dreaded stairs that took you to and from the row where your assigned seat was located. The lecture hall provided a daily buffet, TV sets, and a view of the world's largest indoor scoreboard.

With that improvement, the Augusta National made the USGA and R&A look like slumlords with their crowded press tents. Along with the Masters today, only the PGA of America at its own major constantly strives to enhance our quality of life and typing.

Looking back on it, I recall that I wrote about Ben Hogan and Sam Snead in the old tent, about Arnold Palmer and Jack Nicklaus in the Quonset hut, and about Tiger Woods and Phil Mickelson in the lecture hall.

Trudging forward amid talk of a new facility, I was eager to see what the latest Augusta National pressroom had in store for us. It was rumored to be decadent. When I arrived for the 2017 Masters, the press building's stunning exterior all at once brought to mind Windsor Castle, Versailles, the Biltmore Estate, Twelve Oaks, and Tara.

There it stood in the midst of a grove of beautiful trees and manicured lawns, all of which looked as if they'd been there forever when in fact they'd been planted, placed, and groomed practically overnight.

After entering and touring the indoors, I swooned at the comfort and convenience. Comfortable working spaces were provided for 450 journalists—I remembered how there used to be only thirty or forty of us—with huge TV sets on separate walls and smaller ones at each desk where you sat in swiveling leather armchairs. Through a huge glass vista you could look out at the practice range. There existed a lavish snack bar predictably stocked with the pimento cheese and egg salad sandwiches but with other treats added, and down the hall a real restaurant with smiling waitresses and sumptuous cuisine for breakfast and lunch.

When I'd first entered and was pointed toward the elevator in the lobby that would lift me to the second floor working and dining area, I almost shouted, "Look, no more stairs—I'll live to type another day!"

If a palace guard had been around anywhere, I would have asked him if my bedroom suite was on the same floor as Marie Antoinette's or Scarlett O'Hara's.

On the morning of the first day of the tournament, I couldn't help but reflect on the fact that I alone had achieved the Grand Slam of working in all four Masters press facilities.

And it had only taken seven decades.

Beware: Rascals Loose

WHEN DID so many urchins, scamps, and rascals begin turning up in the galleries of professional golf tournaments? That's one question. Another is, when did the rascals begin to claw and beg for an autograph from any person who bore the slightest resemblance to a touring pro?

I remember my teenage days in the galleries only too well. It started when I was twelve and my dad took me out to Colonial Country Club for the 1941 U.S. Open. I was there for Wednesday's last practice round and all three days of the championship. I was filled with wonderment through it all but disappointed when Craig Wood won instead of Ben Hogan or Byron Nelson, the hometown heroes I'd been told to follow. Hogan did fire the low round of the tournament, a sixty-eight, on Saturday morning, but finished tied for third at the end.

Incidentally, I didn't consider myself an urchin, scamp, or rascal. I'd been playing golf since I was eight and had learned from golfers in my family and by observance that the game was a dignified sport.

If a loon on the course at Colonial had hollered, "You da man," he would have been pounced on by sane people and left to depart in an ambulance.

But that National Open, as it was popularly known at the time, was only the beginning for me.

Three years later I was taken by my Uncle Mack to Lakewood Country Club in Dallas in 1944 to watch Byron Nelson win the Texas Victory Open by a whopping ten strokes over Jug McSpaden, who made me want a pair of tinted aviator glasses like his, and by ten over Lt. Ben Hogan of the US Army Air Corps.

By the age of sixteen, I was driving a car—my uncle had given me his '36 Ford roadster convertible—and I drove myself and two pals to Dallas Country Club in September to watch Sam Snead win the 1945 Dallas

Open over McSpaden with Byron third and Hogan, who was now out of the service, fourth.

Again in '45, I walked every hole with Byron at Glen Garden Country Club in December when he won the Fort Worth Invitational, his eighteenth victory in that record-setting year. He won by eleven shots over Jimmy Demaret.

Onward to 1946, when I stalked Ben Hogan as he won twice. First in the inaugural Colonial National Invitation in May with a course-record sixty-five in the final round, and again in September at the Dallas Invitational on elegant but challenging Brook Hollow Country Club, one of the great courses in the country.

I watched Hogan win another Colonial in '47 and finish second in the '48 Colonial. By then I'd been to eight tour events and I wasn't out of high school yet.

Even then I could recognize how different Ben, Byron, and Sam looked. Ben in his white cap with a smooth flat swing, Byron in his brown visor with a fast upright swing, and Snead in his yellow straw hat with a picture-book swing. The Germans wore gray.

It wasn't as if Ben, Byron, and Sam were beating up on invalids. Aside from Demaret and McSpaden, their competition consisted of such other familiar names as Lloyd Mangrum, Lawson Little, Denny Shute, Henry Picard, Paul Runyan, Vic Ghezzi, Dick Metz, Johnny Bulla, Chick Harbert, Dutch Harrison, Craig Wood, Jimmy Hines, Skip Alexander, Toney Penna, Clayton Heafner, and others.

I've rolled my tournament attendance credits for a reason.

One is to say that in my vast exposure to tournament golf as a youth, I never saw another teenager on the golf courses, much less one impulsive enough to ask a pro for a golf ball. And I can't recall an adult asking a pro for an autograph. It wasn't acceptable. Not in my neck of the woods.

Along with that, applause from the gallery was reserved for a good golf shot. Most of the fans were recreational golfers themselves and were more knowledgeable about the game than most fans in today's throngs.

Nor do I recall any standing ovations for players you've never heard of just because they walked up on a green.

"Come on, Charley, you can do it!"

Who?

What changed this peaceful world?

I'd say Ben Hogan to begin with. The game needed a larger-than-life figure after Bobby Jones retired. Then the timely marriage of Arnold Palmer and TV; the dynasty of Jack Nicklaus; more media attention to the majors—especially the Masters; the growth of new courses, which meant a country club for every income level; advances in equipment; and, yes, a guy named Tiger Woods.

True confession. In my teens, after watching those dapper perfectionists play the game, I did have fleeting thoughts of becoming a pro someday. But by the time I was leading the TCU golf team to less than its share of victories, and not commanding any headlines on the highly competitive Texas amateur circuit in the summers, I realized it would require more practice than I enjoyed, and it would deprive me of too many fun-filled gambling games with friends and thieves on enchanting Goat Hills and other layouts around town.

So I changed my major.

Hogan Takes the Fifth

LET'S GET this out of the way up front. The 1942 Hale America National Open golf tournament that was held at Ridgemoor Country Club in Chicago does, in fact, count as a National Open even though it was a wartime substitute, and when Ben Hogan won the event it gave him the first of his five U.S. Open championships as well as his tenth major, and his ten-under par sixty-two in the second round still stands as the lowest sub-par score ever shot in a major, foreign or domestic, and I hereby rule that any who disagree with these pronouncements should be sentenced to life with a duck hook.

I might add that Ben Hogan agreed with all of the above until his dying day. He often said, "I have a medal that looks like the other four, and if it wasn't a U.S. Open, I don't know what you would call it."

I often lecture on the subject in restaurants and bars and my talk by necessity begins with our entry into World War II. Some of you may have heard about that.

The war was, shall I say, interruptive. It messed with everything, including the world of sports, but we in the USA got off lightly compared to countries where things were falling on people's heads and buildings were turning into rubble.

All of Europe put sports aside when war broke out. Great Britain canceled the British Open for six long years, from '40 through '45. Here, the USGA suspended the "official" National Open for four years, from '42 through '45; the Masters suspended itself from '43 through '45; and the PGA canceled its championship for one year, in '43.

That was it for the majors, which, incidentally, weren't called majors back then. They were known as national championships or "big ones" to the fans and press, and bonus tournaments to the competitors.

116

Equipment and apparel companies rewarded the winners with extra cash and lucrative contracts. And the winners capitalized on their triumphs by endorsing everything from cereal to soda pop to cigarettes.

Which brings to mind a story about Sam Snead and his agent Fred Corcoran. Snead, after winning the '42 PGA—his first major—asked Corcoran why the agent hadn't tried to make a deal for him to advertise a cigarette brand.

Fred said, "You don't smoke, Sam."

Sam said, "What's that got to do with anything?"

In that limited sports year of '43, the PGA Tour consisted of a piddling three individual events. Jug McSpaden won the All-American Open at Tam O'Shanter in Chicago, Sam Byrd won the Chicago Victory Open at Beverly CC, and somebody named Steve Warga Jr. won the Miami Open at Miami Springs. There was one other, the Golden Valley Four-Ball in Minneapolis, where Jimmy Demaret and Craig Wood topped Byron Nelson and McSpaden in a field of eight teams.

All of that went on while Italy was surrendering, Rommel was being chased out of North Africa, and our Marines were taking the island of Guadalcanal from the Japanese after a bloody six-month campaign. In each of the other war years, the tour functioned with a decent schedule of twenty to thirty tournaments, and most of the big names participated.

The first full year of the tour with the war on was '42. Along with Hogan winning the wartime Open, it was the year that certified beyond any doubt that Ben was a force to deal with. He had struggled for seven torturous years to find a way to win, even to stay on the tour, and he'd finally done it in '40 and '41, winning four times in each of those seasons. And he'd kept it up as '42 got underway. He roared out of the box to win the Los Angeles Open—richest event of the year—and the San Francisco Open, the prestigious North and South Open, the Asheville Open, and he barely lost the Masters by one stroke to Byron Nelson, his Fort Worth buddy, in a classic playoff, Byron firing a sixty-nine to Ben's seventy. Of course he still hadn't won a "big one," but that moment was waiting for him around the corner.

The '42 Open had been scheduled for Interlachen Country Club in Minneapolis, one of the four courses on which Bobby Jones had won the Grand Slam twelve years earlier. But not long after the attack on Pearl

Harbor on December 7, 1941, Interlachen begged off holding the Open. There was a war on, you see.

Thus it happened that Ridgemoor Country Club offered to host a "wartime" National Open for the benefit of the Navy Relief Society and the USO. The club chose its name for the event from a slogan on a patriotic poster: "Stay Hale and Hearty, Keep America Fit."

Ridgemoor's offer sounded like a good idea—and a salute to patriotism—to the USGA, which controlled the rules of the game, to the PGA of America, which ran the Tour in those days, and to the Chicago District Golf Association, which could round up the tournament volunteers. The three organizations agreed to co-sponsor the tournament, and the USGA was asked to run it as closely as possible to a regular National Open.

ENTER JOSEPH C. DEY JR. He was the executive secretary of the USGA for a period of thirty-four years, from '34 through '68. He was a rigid gentleman with an aristocratic manner who took his job to the far side of seriously. We used to joke that Joe never listened to a player ask for relief from an unfair or inconvenient lie in an Open that he didn't respond with the same two words: "Hit it."

The first thing Joe did was declare that to be a proper event, it should hold local and sectional qualifying throughout the country, as was the case with regular U.S. Opens. The result was a record number of entries—1,541. Dey next ordained that prize money should be the same as previous U.S. Opens, meaning $1,000 to the champion, and the winner would receive the same gold medal that other National Open champions had been given in the past.

Joe became a friend and helpful in my job through the years, and I enjoyed teasing him about having such deep respect for the Open title that he wanted the host course set up so cursedly impossible, nobody could win it.

But the lack of manpower due to the war effort prevented Ridgemoor from receiving the full USGA treatment, meaning that Joe couldn't narrow the fairways to the width of a pants leg, grow the rough deep enough to swallow a FootJoy, or shave the greens down to the speed of "Merion lightning" or "Oakmont ice."

Ridgemoor was a balanced layout of 36-36-72, but it was nevertheless unique. It presented back-to-back par fives on the outgoing nine, the second and third, and back-to-back par fives on the incoming nine, the fourteenth and fifteenth, and it closed with a water-guarded 175-yard par three. There hadn't been a par-three eighteenth hole in an Open since Englewood Country Club in New Jersey in 1909. And there hasn't been one since. That's if you're wondering.

Ridgemoor's length was okay at 6,519 yards. That length was in the ballpark of other U.S. Open courses of the era, but if anything the thick, shaggy, inconsistently tailored fairways made it play longer—the competitors found that achieving any roll on their drives was virtually impossible.

Hogan said in later years that Ridgemoor's uneven fairways were the course's best defense—and a problem. He recalled, "You had to invent a new shot in every fairway."

The field numbered 107, of whom ninety-six were qualifiers. A few "names" were invited to help sell tickets, and did participate. This list included Bobby Jones, Walter Hagen, Jock Hutchison, Chick Evans, and—yes—Bing Crosby, who was a scratch amateur then. Other bells and whistles were added to help draw a crowd and raise money for the war effort. There was no thirty-six-hole cut, pairings were a combination of scores and whim, and they played four days instead of three.

But as Ron Sirak, my friend and journalism colleague—himself a stern campaigner for Hogan's fifth Open—has written in regard to the Hale America, "If it walks like a U.S. Open, and talks like a U.S. Open, why isn't it a U.S. Open?"

HOGAN DIDN'T EXACTLY start off in a blaze. His par seventy-two in the first round left him in a tie for forty-ninth place. The lead was shared by two journeymen pros, Mike Turnesa, a member of the golfing Turnesa family, and Otey Crisman, who would become a bigger name after the war for the popular mallet-style putter he designed and marketed. They shot seven-under par sixty-fives.

In Ben's historic second round, he was again paired with Tommy Armour, the Silver Scot, winner of three majors in the past, who was now forty-six years old, and Corp. Vic Ghezzi, on leave from the Army, the '41 PGA champion. That day Ben shot the record sixty-two to climb back into the tournament, pulling himself up to within three strokes of Turnesa, who led by himself at 131.

Ben's epic round consisted of eight birdies, one eagle, and no bogies, and he barely lipped out a makeable birdie putt on eighteen that would have given him a sixty-one!

Armour said, "Ben's round was more workmanlike than sensational. He just made the game look simple all the way around, which we know it isn't."

Hogan's sixty-two and his move into contention indeed brought out the crowds. A record twelve thousand turned up for each of the last two days. It didn't matter that the third round was played in rain, mist, and fog. Ben's sixty-nine equaled the day's best on Saturday and placed him in a tie for the lead with Mike Turnesa at 203. But other marquee gents were hanging close. Jimmy Demaret was only two back, Horton Smith was three behind, and Byron Nelson was within range at five back.

The cosponsors included a touch of show biz to Sunday's final round. They paired Hogan with Bobby Jones, or I should say Capt. Robert T. Jones, on leave from the United States Army, Hogan wearing a loose-fitting long-sleeve sports shirt with the collar buttoned and his familiar white cap, and Jones no longer in a shirt, necktie, and plus fours but in a crewneck slipover short-sleeve golf shirt and a floppy-brim hat. Hogan and Jones went out in the group directly behind Demaret and Turnesa.

As the saying goes, somebody has to lose a National Open before somebody else can win it.

Jimmy Demaret filled that role. Demaret had shot his way to a two-stroke lead on the field with just four holes to play, largely with the aid of holing out a second shot at thirteen for an eagle deuce. But the Open nerves got him. He bogied the fifteenth when he jerked his drive and wound up behind a tree, suffered another bogey at the sixteenth after his second shot hit a spectator, and three-putted the seventeenth for yet another bogey before the bleeding stopped.

Taking advantage of the opportunity, Hogan fired two birdies to pick up five strokes on Demaret over the last four holes, the final blow coming on a twenty-five-foot birdie putt that Ben sank on the eighteenth green for a sixty-eight.

Hogan wound up winning by three shots over Demaret and Turnesa, who tied for second, and by seven over Byron Nelson, Horton Smith, and long-hitting Jimmy Thomson, all of whom tied for fourth.

The world knows that Hogan went on to win four "official" National Opens at Riviera in Los Angeles, Merion in Philadelphia, Oakland Hills in Detroit, and Oakmont in Pittsburgh, giving him the same total as Bobby Jones, Jack Nicklaus, and Willie Anderson.

The question remains for others as to whether the "wartime" Open should count as Hogan's fifth, breaking him out of that four-way deadlock.

Myself and other Hoganistas insist that the only real difference between the event at Ridgemoor and the official Opens is the engraving on the back of the gold medals. On the official four, it says, "Open Championship" and lists the year, course, city, and winner. On the Ridgemoor medal, which was presented to Hogan by the president of the US Golf Association, it says "Hale America National Open Tournament" and lists the year, course, city, and winner.

As for the questionable difficulty of Ridgemoor producing Hogan's winning total of 271, one might ask today if Pebble Beach in 2000 was up to Open standards when Tiger Woods shot twelve under 272 to win by fifteen strokes, or more to the point if Congressional in 2011 was up to Open standards when Rory McIlroy shot a sixteen under 268, breaking the 270 barrier for the first time, and winning by eight strokes.

Some years ago when Joe Dey was still among us, I had a long chat with him about the Hale America and why, to me, it should count as Ben Hogan's fifth U.S. Open.

Joe said, "Nobody was a bigger fan of Ben than I was, and I would like nothing better than to call it his fifth Open championship. But because of the manpower shortage caused by the war, we couldn't prepare the course properly, and that's the main reason the USGA doesn't count it as an official Open."

Joe paused for moment, then he added:

"But I *do* call it a major."

Excuse me?

Hogan Lives On

YOUR CORRESPONDENT freely admits that he surrendered to attacks of whimsical thought and has hereby exaggerated the actual exchanges with these daunting tradesmen in golf memorabilia. But don't let this stop you from reading.

Since aging golf items are now worth more than your stash of gold coins, you need to look carefully at the proposals that come your way and be alert enough to separate the relic scammers from the legitimate dealers and collectors.

There are these tricksters in the world who will try to sell you a tooth that was jarred loose from Gene Sarazen's mouth when he hit the four-wood shot that went into the cup for a double eagle in the '35 Masters. You might even be offered the wrinkled golf glove worn by Sam Snead when he made the tragic eight on the last hole at Spring Mill that cost him the '39 National Open.

But memorabilia quickens the collector's pace when it applies to Ben Hogan. Any entrepreneur worth his weight in persimmon knows that an item that once belonged to Hogan comes with dollar signs dancing around it.

Within the past year I've received proposals that literally cried out for a response.

Here's a dandy:

> Dear Sir: Knowing you are a fan of Ben Hogan, I have something that might be of financial interest to you. It has to do with a pair of golf shoes.
>
> You are of course aware that when Hogan won the U S Open at Merion in 1950, his golf shoes and 1-iron were stolen that night before the next day's 18-hole playoff with Lloyd Mangrum and George Fazio. Hogan

admitted he never learned what became of them. I happen to know where the shoes are. I am looking at them.

I acquired these treasures from a man in Mississippi who was given the shoes in payment for a gambling debt by the son of the person who stole the shoes. Only the shoes, not the 1-iron. The club was stolen by someone else, I assume. I met the gentleman with the shoes at a poker table in a Biloxi casino.

During a breather, he mentioned the shoes he now owned. I was flabbergasted. I paid him $5,000 for the shoes, knowing they were worth much more than that.

Three collectors have authenticated them for me. The shoes are two-toned brown and white saddle oxfords. They are Hogan's shoe size of 8-1/2 C, and they have the extra spike on the soles. Do I hear an offer?

My response:

No. And here's why. Ben Hogan rarely wore two-tone golf shoes during the 1950s—his peak years. By then, he could afford to have his shoes specially made in London and New York. He preferred solid colors. White, brown, and black. He traveled with several pair and may have worn two-tone shoes in a practice round at Merion. But the shoes that were stolen were solid white. By the way, Ben's exact shoe size was 9-B. And the bottoms contained TWO extra spikes to give him better traction in his stance. One on the sole and one on the heel. Ben had this done by a cobbler at Wilkerson Shoe Repair on the east side of Fort Worth.

I hope the golf shoes fit your own feet.

Here's another one:

Hello. I have a story to tell you about a putter. You may or may not know that when Ben Hogan won the 1953 United States Open at Oakmont, he gave his putter away as a keepsake to an elderly man in a wheelchair who was sitting behind the ropes on the 18th green.

The elderly man proudly kept the putter displayed in his garage until his death in 1967. The putter fell into the possession of his nephew, a struggling golf pro, who was not a church-going individual.

Hoping the putter would bring him luck, the nephew used it trying to qualify on a course in Houston for the 1975 U. S. Open. But he

3-putted eight times on the front nine, lost his temper, and tossed the club into a pond. His caddie waded in and rescued it, thinking it might be valuable someday.

The putter apparently changed hands many times after that, but it was brought to me recently by an acquaintance in Dallas who had purchased it from a gentleman in Las Vegas. I only had to feel the offset grip and stare at the etchings on the bottom to know I was holding history in my hands.

I paid him $20,000 for the putter. Now I'm looking for a partner who may have more contacts in the golf world than I do. You can buy in for $15,000. I suggest we start the bidding at $50,000. The putter is, after all, Ben Hogan's durable old Bulls Eye.

My response:

Thanks, but I can only offer you a history lesson. If Hogan ever putted with a Bulls Eye it must have been in the middle 1940s when the putter first went on sale, and only then out of curiosity. Ben won all of his majors with a putter hand-crafted out of a brass doorknob and given to him by Ky Laffoon, another tour player of some renown.

Today that authentic "doorknob" putter resides safely in the Ben Hogan Room at the USGA headquarters and museum in Far Hills, New Jersey.

And one more:

Hi, I am a devoted searcher of golf memorabilia and I have been on the trail of Ben Hogan's stolen 1-iron for years. I once tracked it from Bucharest to Marseilles, to Barcelona, to Lisbon, and on to San Francisco by tramp steamer, and finally to New York City by rail.

All this while the 1-iron passed from one unsavory character to another. But I finally located it in the shop of a certain antiquities dealer on the corner of 83rd Street and Lexington Avenue. I now own it.

Having researched the history of you and Ben Hogan, I am pleased to offer you this club for only $75,000. It has been examined by experts and I am informed that it is authentic.

The 1-iron shows its age and although the signature is scratchy it is clearly Ben Hogan's name engraved on the back of the face. It definitely comes from a set of early Ben Hogan Precision Irons. Can't wait to hear back from you.

My response:

While I was entertained by your tale of trying to track down "The Maltese 1-Iron," I am compelled to inform you that the club stolen at Merion was made by MacGregor. Hogan played MacGregor clubs to win all of his majors. The Ben Hogan Company did not begin marketing clubs until late in 1953. Ben did win three tournaments using his own Hogan Company clubs—the 1956 World Cup individual and team title (with Sam Snead) at Wentworth in England, and the 1959 Colonial National Invitational.

But the golf club in your possession has definitely performed one of the most amazing feats in sports. That particular 1-iron somehow managed to help Hogan hit an epic shot and win a U.S. Open four years before it existed.

Good luck with any other items you may have to sell, including your original, authenticated copy of the Magna Carta.

A Personal Farewell

THE FIRST TIME I paid any attention to Arnold Palmer he was standing on the veranda at the Masters on a day in 1957, and I wondered who that visiting coal miner was and where he'd lost the headlamp off his cap.

I was aware that a guy by his name had been on the tour for a while and had won three or four events, but so had a bunch of other pros who were majorless. And walking around majorless is never a good thing to be where the press is concerned.

Arnold had been visiting with my pal Bob Drum, a sportswriter from Pittsburgh, who'd known Palmer since he was a teenager. A little later, Drum informed me, "That was Arnold D. Palmer of Latrobe, Pennsylvania, the next great player."

"Yeah, right," I said.

Drum said, "You can book it. He hits it a mile. He makes 4,567 birdies a week. One day he'll eliminate the bogeys, and he'll knock off Venturi, Littler, Souchak, Casper, Sanders. Arnold Palmer is the next great chin."

Usually when Drum spoke, you listened. He was larger than two Porky Olivers, stacked. He was unrelentingly Irish, he could outdrink the British army and not lose a step, and he was one of the most entertaining people you'd ever meet in or around sports—if you could take a ribbing.

It's impossible to reminisce about Arnold Palmer without including Drum in the conversation. Bob and I became friends in 1951. I was covering my first Masters and we were accidentally seated next to one another in the old press tent.

How could I not have become friends with a guy who'd type a paragraph, and lean back to laugh at what he'd written?

In those golden days we joked that there were only two golfers, Ben Hogan and Sam Snead. Most golf writers are strict about touring pros having marquee names. As I've mentioned, our bosses tended to blame us if we allowed an Ed Furgol or a Jack Fleck to win a major.

CERTAIN WRITERS in the old days often claimed ownership of accomplished golfers, as O. B. Keeler of the *Atlanta Journal* had once owned Bobby Jones.

I was lucky to claim Hogan when I was with the *Fort Worth Press*. Hogan was the reason I began covering the majors in the first place. I'd follow Ben shot by shot, but cover the championship as well. In that same period, early on—and before Palmer—Drum was partial to Sam Snead. We would share quotes. Drum knew Snead better than I did, and I obviously knew Hogan better than Bob.

There was the day I asked Bob what Snead had said after he tracked down Sam in the clubhouse while I was typing.

Drum said, "Sam was funny, but you can't print any of it in a family paper."

"Gee, that's helpful," I said. And I quoted Drum's exact words regarding the Slammer.

But I got even. It was after Hogan arranged for me to stay in the Richmond Hotel in downtown Augusta for a number of years during the Masters. The Richmond was the best lodge in town. It was where Ben and Valerie stayed. Drum thought this gave me even more of an insight into Hogan.

I *was* invited to join Ben and Valerie for dinner in the Richmond dining room a couple of times, but mostly they stayed in their suite, ordered dinner from room service, and played gin rummy.

One day Drum asked me what Hogan said last night. I told him Ben had said, "Gin!"

ARNOLD WAS THE GUY we were waiting for. Hogan and Snead would never win another major after 1954, although you couldn't tell this to the monster galleries they attracted throughout the decade.

Palmer became the most likable and helpful athlete any of us had covered in any sport. Part of his attraction was that he fought a golf course. He sweated. His shirttail came out. He chain-smoked. He tried to drive the golf ball through dense forests. He sank improbable putts to rescue himself from trouble or sculpt a low round. All of that was appealing to the masses as well as the scribes.

Even after he was done winning he never refused to sign autographs for admirers. I once offered to buy him a set of binoculars so he could scan the crowds and maybe find one more person who had something for him to sign.

It was in 1960 he became whoo-ha Arnie, golf's miracle man.

At Augusta in that year's first major, he ran in birdie putts over the final two holes to edge Ken Venturi by a stroke and win his second Masters. It was suspenseful. They'd traded the lead back and forth over the last thirty-six holes.

Drum and I had different chores on our papers. I was writing a lead, column, and sidebar every day while Bob was only writing a feature. So he went alone to catch Palmer and collect quotes for us.

"What did he say?" I asked when Bob returned to the press room, which was now the funky Quonset hut. Bob quoted Arnold saying the Augusta National played like a par sixty-eight, and he was going to enter the British Open—he'd decided the modern Grand Slam should be the Masters, U.S. Open, British Open, and PGA.

"*Arnold Palmer* said all that?"

"No, Laurie Auchterlonie said it. Who are we talking about?"

On to the '60 U.S. Open at Cherry Hills. Greatest last day of the Open, ever. I feel I've written about it too many times, but I'll try it once more.

Drum and I were in the locker room between the third and fourth rounds on Saturday. The Open was still contested over thirty-six holes on the last day then. Mike Souchak was leading. Palmer was seven strokes and fourteen players behind. It looked like he had about as much chance to win as Macdonald Smith, who was dead.

Arnold stopped to visit on his way out for the last eighteen. The first hole at Cherry Hills, a slightly downhill 346-yard par four, was bugging him.

"I ought to be able to drive that green," he said. "I've come close."

"Sure," said Drum. "If you hire a limousine."

Arnold looked at both of us. "You coming out?"

Drum said, "I'm tired of watching duck hooks. There's a guy named Souchak leading. He's from Pittsburgh, too."

Palmer said, "If I drive the first green and get a birdie or an eagle, I might shoot sixty-five."

"Good," Drum said. "You'll finish fourteenth."

Arnold said, "A sixty-five will give me 280. Doesn't 280 always win the Open?"

"Yeah, when Hogan shoots it," I said with a grin.

Arnold laughed and went out the door.

The rest is history. Arnold drove the first green and two-putted for a birdie. He birdied six of the first seven holes. By then Drum and I were out on the course watching Palmer shoot that sixty-fve and win the Open, barely edging out Jack Nicklaus and Ben Hogan in a stirring drama. I was brilliant enough to recognize it as a battle between the current king, the future king, and the past king.

Cut to 1962 where Arnold was talking about the Grand Slam again after winning the Masters in a playoff over Gary Player and Dow Finsterwald. Now he headed into the U.S. Open at Oakmont in Pittsburgh, a course he knew almost as well as he knew Winnie.

But too many three-putt greens cost him that Open to Jack Nicklaus. Drum and I caught up with Arnold in the parking lot after their eighteen-hole playoff, where Jack topped him seventy-one to seventy-four. Arnold was gracious at the prize ceremony, but now he was beating himself up.

"Tough loss," Drum said.

"Best I've ever played," Arnold said. "I can't believe the way I messed up the ninth yesterday. It's a gimme birdie, but I flub a chip and miss it from one foot for par—there shouldn't have been a damn playoff."

"You three-putted eleven times," I said. "Jack only once."

Drum said, "Screw statistics. The fat kid can chin it."

Palmer said, "I can beat the fat kid the best day he ever had."

THREE WEEKS LATER Arnold beat Nicklaus and everyone else in the field to win the British Open at Troon by six strokes. Drum and I were there—it was my first British Open. I was fascinated by everything. The atmosphere, the fans, the heather, gorse, bracken, broom, sausage rolls, pork pies.

We were invited to celebrate with Arnold and Winnie at dinner in the Marine Hotel dining room. Others in the room took turns standing up to toast Arnold. At one point the staff brought a cake to Palmer at our table with an inscription in icing that said, "Open Champion."

Arnold sliced the cake, took a piece, stood up, smiled at the well-wishers in the room, and sat back down. Then to the three of us, he quietly said, "Do you suppose I have to eat it?"

Arnold beat "the fat kid" one more time in a major. That was in the 1964 Masters. It was a drowning. He won by six over Nicklaus and Dave Marr—they finished in a tie for second. It would be Palmer's fourth Masters, but it would also be remembered for Dave Marr's immortal quip.

Arnold was paired with his good friend Marr in the last round, and as he stood on the tee at the seventy-second hole, enjoying his comfortable lead, he turned to him and said, "Anything I can do to help you here, Dave?"

Marr said, "Yeah. Make a twelve."

Arnold never won another major, but it seemed like he did. He threatened constantly and finished runner-up in five more. Overall, he was second in ten majors to go along with his seven wins.

There was a moment before his winning days were over when Drum and I were visiting with him in Latrobe. We were admiring the coffee table he'd had made to display the gold medals he'd won in the majors and the regular tour events. But among them were the four silver medals for his second-place finishes in the U.S. Open.

I said to Arnold, "What are these silver ones doing in here?"

He said, "They're not exactly ugly."

WHEN ARNOLD PASSED AWAY in 2016, I was as saddened as the rest of the sports world—and flooded with memories.

The last time I'd seen him was a year earlier on the Augusta National veranda after he'd hit his ceremonial tee shot at the Masters. We shook hands warmly and didn't say much. Our looks said it all. It had been quite a trip for both of us.

Twenty years earlier, in 1996, I'd enjoyed my last lunch with Bob Drum upstairs in the Augusta National clubhouse. A place where we'd dined so often over forty-five years.

We both knew it was Bob's last Augusta. He was ill then and surrendered to a heart attack a little over a month later at his home in Pinehurst.

Bob said that day at lunch, "We beat the game, pal, but we never got any respect."

I said, "Why didn't we get any respect?"

He said, "We sat around and laughed too much."

Another Stroll
Down Memory Lane

WHEN I FIRST STARTED writing about golf for a living, I could never have imagined that someday I'd become the Ancient Twitterer of the Game. But when I went to the 2017 PGA Championship in Charlotte, it was my 230th major to cover, and it occurred to me that over the years I'd gone from hammering out 2,500-word stories on deadline to creating 140-character tweets.

You might guess that I've seen so many majors they've become a blur of green jackets, USGA rulings, and dodging plates of haggis. However, I've clung to memories of the best of them, in particular those that were won by headliners as opposed to your basic lurkers.

For this exercise, I've narrowed my faves down to the four most memorable in each decade, those I've observed with my own eyes, typed with my own fingers, and tweeted with my own mind.

1950-59:

The '51 Masters was my first major to cover and Ben Hogan's first Masters to win. I'd never seen a golf course that green, or blue ponds, or pine trees so tall. In those days the Masters paired by whim rather than by scores. So Hogan went out on Sunday two hours behind the coleaders, Sam Snead and Skee Riegel, but Ben cruised home with a four-under sixty-eight, the only sub-seventy round of the day, to win by two strokes.

Oakland Hills at the '51 U.S. Open is still the most punishing golf course ever inflicted on mankind. It featured calf-deep rough, bunkers in the middle of fairways, and greens faster than marble. Hogan started the final round two strokes and four players behind, but that layout was where he shot his historic sixty-seven to win. At the trophy ceremony, Ben said, "I'm glad I could bring this monster to its knees." In the locker room he called it something else.

In his Triple Crown year, Hogan led all the way in the '53 U.S. Open at Oakmont, although Snead stayed close. Ben went out an hour ahead of Sam in the final round, and he was standing on the seventieth tee when he learned that Snead was only one back with nine to play. Ben solved that problem by finishing 3-3-3, a par and two birdies to demoralize Sam and win by six.

The Masters of '54 remains as thrilling as any. It marked the last time that Hogan and Snead would duke it out in a major. Sam won their eighteen-hole playoff seventy to seventy-one, largely due to a chip-in birdie that skittered all the way across the old rye green at the tenth hole.

But the tournament was dominated by an unknown amateur, Billy Joe Patton. Billy Joe led the first two rounds, fell back, but reclaimed the lead on Sunday with a hole-in-one at No. 6. Yeah, an ace. Then just as shockingly, he gave away the green jacket with a double bogey at the par-five thirteenth hole, and lost by one. Hogan himself gave it away on Sunday when he pulled his second shot at No. 11 into the water for a double bogey. Which left him to say, "If you ever see me near the pin on No. 11 again, you'll know I hit a bad shot."

1960-69:

The greatest last day of any U.S. Open is still 1960 at Cherry Hills in Denver, the day that Arnold Palmer outlasted Ben Hogan and Jack Nicklaus. Arnold's closing six-under sixty-five brought him the trophy, but he still needed a little help. He got it from Hogan, who, while tied for the lead after hitting thirty-four greens in regulation, fatted a pitch shot into the water on the seventy-first hole for a bogey, and Nicklaus three-putted twice for bogies over the last five holes. But maybe Palmer caused some of that misfortune.

By the time the U.S. Open returned to Oakmont in '62, Arnold Palmer had won five majors. He towered over the sport. But his local knowledge of Oakmont did him little good as he three-putted his way into a tie with a young Jack Nicklaus, who had turned pro that year. Jack's power game overwhelmed Palmer. Nicklaus constantly outdrove him by an average of thirty yards and won the playoff seventy-one to seventy-four. It was the start of something.

Palmer played some of the best golf of his life after Oakmont. He trampled Troon in the '62 British Open, winning by six shots and capturing the heart of every Scot. Arnold spectacularly played Troon's eleventh hole, "The Railway," a long, narrow par-four with out of bounds close on the right, arguably the toughest hole in all of Scotland, in two-under par for the tournament.

Now came Lee Trevino—Super Mex—to liven up the sports pages. A product of public course gambling games around Dallas, Lee won the '68 U.S. Open at Oak Hill in Rochester by crushing the three-day leader Bert Yancey and becoming the first Open winner to shoot all four rounds in the sixties. Lee celebrated by saying, "I'm gonna buy the Alamo and redecorate it."

1970-79:

Here was a decade ruled by marquee names. Nicklaus won eight majors, starting with the '70 British Open at St. Andrews, an exciting event from start to finish, topped off by Jack driving the par-four eighteenth green and getting down in two for the birdie that defeated Doug Sanders seventy-two to seventy-three in the playoff.

It was in '72 that Nicklaus became only the fourth competitor to win the Masters and U.S. Open, the year's first two majors. Craig Wood, Ben Hogan, and Arnold Palmer had done it before him, Hogan twice. Only two have done it since, Tiger Woods and Jordan Spieth.

This set up a tough loss for Nicklaus. On an incredible last day of golf in the British Open at Muirfield, Jack chased Lee Trevino and Tony Jacklin and closed with a blazing sixty-six. He lost by a stroke to Trevino, who chipped in for a birdie from off the seventy-first green. In typical fashion, Trevino said, "I didn't come over here to help Jack Nicklaus win the Grand Slam."

The '75 Masters produced a dramatic finish. Nicklaus found himself in a day-long battle with Johnny Miller and Tom Weiskopf. Jack held them off by hitting one of the great pressure shots of his career, a 2-iron to No. 15 to secure a two-putt birdie. And he followed that at No. 16 by sinking one of the timeliest putts of his career—a forty-foot birdie that seemed to take forever to reach the cup.

Perhaps as jolting to Nicklaus as his narrow loss to Trevino at Muirfield was his narrow loss to Tom Watson in the '77 British Open at Turnberry. That's where Jack shot the final thirty-six holes in 65-66 only to have Watson shoot 65-65. Hubert Green finished third a mile back, and said, "I won the British Open. I don't know what tournament Tom and Jack were playing." The decisive blow was Watson's speeding thirty-foot birdie putt from off the green at the sixty-ninth hole that struck the flagstick, which kept it from continuing on to France.

Bonus pick: Seve Ballesteros won his first of five majors in the '79 British Open at Royal Lytham & St. Annes. Forever wild off the tee, this was where Seve was given a free drop from a parking lot near No. 15 in the last round, and he turned it into the birdie that enabled him to fight off Jack Nicklaus and Ben Crenshaw, thereby earning his nickname, "the Car Park Champion."

1980-89:

Tom Watson became the great escape artist in the last round of the '82 U.S. Open at Pebble Beach. He sank a twenty-five-foot putt to save par, rolled in a forty-foot putt for a birdie, and pulled off that fabulous chip-in at the seventy-first green for the birdie that slammed the door on Nicklaus. Jack played some of his best golf ever that week, tee to green, but he had to deal with an obstinate putter. In the end, it was just another of Jack's nineteen runner-up finishes in the majors.

It seemed like every member of the press rejoiced when Ben Crenshaw finally won a major, the '84 Masters. It had taken him eleven years on the tour and five second places in majors to do it. After leading with a first round sixty-seven, Ben fell behind by four at thirty-six, and was two behind at fifty-four, but a closing sixty-eight overtook the field on Sunday and nipped Tom Watson at the wire.

The '86 Masters stands alone. It was where Jack Nicklaus won his sixth green jacket and his record eighteenth professional major at the age of forty-six. And what a final round it was. Jack's needed every stroke of his closing seven-under sixty-five to win in a firefight with Tom Watson, Greg Norman, Seve Ballesteros, Nick Price, and Tom Kite—a virtual Hall of Fame. It was epic. It was historic. It was sentimental.

It's a short list of guys who have won back-to-back U.S. Opens. But the '89 Open at Oak Hill was where Curtis Strange joined Willie Anderson, John McDermott, Bobby Jones, Ralph Guldahl, and Ben Hogan in doing so. That week in Rochester, the course became known as "Soak Hill." It was drenched from the start through the third round, at which point Strange, who had won at the Country Club in Boston the previous summer, trailed the leading Tom Kite by three.

This was where Curtis slogged his way to a closing seventy that was good enough for a one-stroke victory over three unexpected contenders, Ian Woosnam, Chip Beck, and Mark McCumber. Kite found all sorts of trouble the last day and his line score read like a typo: 67-69-69-78.

1990-1999:

Hale Irwin did a quaint thing. He started the decade by winning his third U.S. Open at Medinah in Chicago. The '90 Open is best remembered for Hale's forty-five-foot birdie putt on the seventy-second green and his victory lap that followed. But he had to beat Mike Donald in a playoff to hoist the trophy. Two playoffs, actually. They were still tied after eighteen holes, but Hale dropped a ten-foot birdie putt on the first sudden-death hole. Irwin remains the only pro to confine his three majors to U.S. Open titles.

Nick Faldo and Greg Norman were the dominant players of the nineties with Faldo's wins and Norman's near-wins. While Nick played steady fairways-and-greens golf and was rewarded for it, Greg played flamboyant golf but at times self-destructed. He suffered an inordinate amount of bad luck as well. Except for one week in the '93 British Open at Sandwich. In the heat of battle, Norman's final round 64 and his record-breaking 267 total outlasted Faldo by two strokes. It was Greg's finest hour.

A year later, Ernie Els, the Big Easy, burst on the scene in the '94 U.S. Open at Oakmont to win the first of his four majors. Ernie took advantage of a controversial USGA ruling—relief from an immovable object that wasn't—and then won the Open in a playoff over Loren Roberts and Colin Montgomerie. Oh, and it was the week of the O. J. Bronco chase.

Another explosion happened to the game when a young Tiger Woods dominated the '97 Masters. He did the impossible, playing seventy-two holes on the Augusta National's undulating greens without a three-putt. This enabled him to set a new tournament record of 270 and win by twelve strokes. It was the first of Tiger's fourteen majors. For eight years, he would be golf's only rock star.

2000-2009:

The millennium arrived to find Tiger dominating the tour but ultimately peaking out, to put it nicely. He did win twelve majors in the decade, and none more confidently than the way he stomped on Pebble Beach in the 2000 U.S. Open. He opened with a sixty-five and cruised to a fifteen-stroke win over Ernie Els and Miguel Angel Jimenez. You can't do that to Pebble.

After winning the British Open at St. Andrews by eight shots over the same Ernie Els in addition to Denmark's Thomas Bjorn, Tiger completed the second Triple Crown in golf history (after Hogan in '53). It was finalized at the 2000 PGA at Valhalla in Louisville, although not easily. An obscure Bob May, the greatest lurker since Sam Parks Jr., tied Tiger with a final round sixty-six and took the rock star to a three-hole playoff where Tiger survived with a birdie and two pars.

Another welcomed story was Phil Mickelson doing something his followers had been waiting years for him to do: win a major. Phil did it in the 2004 Masters, and did it in style. He birdied five of the last seven holes to edge Ernie Els by one shot. Which happened to be the eighteen-foot birdie putt Phil holed on the final green. To date, it holds up as the longest winning putt in Masters history.

The weird 2005 PGA at Baltusrol in New Jersey saw Mickelson capture his second major. It required another final-hole performance—a fifty-foot lob-chip out of high grass to two feet of the cup for the birdie that beat Steve Elkington and Thomas Bjorn by one stroke, and Tiger Woods and Dave Love III by two. But this was on Monday morning after Sunday's play was suspended by rain—and Tiger had taken a powder. Flown home. He'd completed his seventy-two holes before the downpour and departed, even though he stood a chance to win depending on what Mickelson, Elk, Bjorn, Love, and two others did on their remaining holes. A curious thing for anyone to do, was it not?

2010-2017:

Enter the Boy King from Northern Ireland, Rory McIlroy. He had thrown away three excellent chances to win majors before he broke through in the 2011 U.S. Open at Congressional in DC, where he won by eight strokes over Jason Day. It was a clinic. It almost made up for the Masters he blew with an eighty in the last round highlighted by a triple bogey at No. 10 when he hooked his tee shot onto the doorstep of one of the private cottages.

Phil again. He roared out of the pack in the last round of the 2013 British Open at Muirfield with a five-under sixty-six that brought him from five strokes and eight players behind to win his fifth major. Among those Phil passed as he birdied four of the last six grueling holes were Tiger Woods, Adam Scott, Henrik Stenson, and Lee Westwood. No doubt it was Phil's greatest triumph in a long career that's seen him finish second in eleven majors. You'd think two or three of those would have accidentally landed in his lap.

The 2014 PGA at Valhalla is the only major I've covered that ended in the dark. But that only added to the drama. It was also the most exciting PGA Championship I've covered. The last round introduced a log-floater that flooded the layout. How the course drained off those rivers and became playable again that day was a miracle. But when attention shifted back to golf, we were treated to Rory McIlroy's nerve-testing win over Mickelson, the old silver collector, in a dash against darkness. Having taken the British Open a month earlier at Hoylake, the win gave McIlroy his fourth major.

Yet it was only a year later that Rory surrendered his Boy King title to a twenty-one-year-old Texan, Jordan Spieth, who startled the world by winning the Masters with a seventy-two-hole total of 270 that tied Tiger's record. Spieth's popularity grew as he added a win in the 2015 U.S. Open at Chambers Bay with a closing birdie and seriously challenged for the British Open and PGA. Jordan's finishes in the Grand Slam events for the year read 1-1-4-2, which is about as good as you can do without the names of Jones, Hogan, and Tiger coming up.

Bonus pick: Spieth's incomparable win at Royal Birkdale in the 2017 British Open, his third major at the age of twenty-three. He won it for three rounds, lost it briefly to Matt Kuchar in the last round by stumbling to three-over par through twelve holes, but somehow fought back. Jordan's foul frame of mind must have been the kind from which 99 percent of all golfers never recover. But he scrambled and made "the bogey that won the Open" at No. 13, and followed that with a miraculous streak of birdie-eagle-birdie-birdie-par—five-under over the last five holes—to grab the trophy out of the clutches of a hapless Kuchar.

I confess to tweeting that one from home on TV. My heart doctor had ordered me to avoid overseas travel from now on. Which is disappointing, but I'm resigned to it. I covered a total of forty-five British Opens.

And that's enough bubble and squeak, neeps and tatties, and pork pies for one American chap.

Tennis, No One?

WHAT'S HAPPENED TO TENNIS? It seems to have disappeared before my very eyes, like Yugoslavia.

Today we're frequently offered Milo Radwanska vs. Daxtra Kojanovich in a men's Grand Slam final and Grushenka Muskinova vs. Tamara Nostradamus in a women's Grand Slam final.

Does anyone else miss Rod Laver?

Billie Jean King?

Chrissie vs. Martina?

McEnroe vs. Borg?

Steffi?

On the men's tour these days you're likely to look around at any moment and see where a guy with a name like a nasal spray, Nadal, or a guy with a name like a kitchen utensil, del Potro, was paid $3 million dollars for conquering a lineup of nobodies at the International Black Sea Lamborghini Potato Vodka Classic in a village somewhere near the Bosphorus.

Who cares?

It's mildly amusing to me that tennis stars think they're succeeding in a rich man's sport. But if they could see beyond their next expo fee, they'd realize that yachting, horse racing, buying countries, and owning politicians are the sports of the wealthy. Tennis is a middle-class sport.

I don't pin this rap on an institution like Roger Federer, who won his eighth Wimbledon at the decrepit age of thirty-six. All Roger has done is play the game so well he's made it look dull. The only suspense with Federer is wondering if he will ever decide how he wants to spell his last name.

Over on the female side, there's Serena Williams. She's done her best to kill women's tennis by beating everyone to a pulp. I suspect this stems from a deep anger within. She is unable to find a Broadway producer who'll let her star in a remake of *Ziegfeld Girl*.

THE SPORT almost put itself to rest for me a year ago at Wimbledon when I tried to interview Igor Yommick, "the Pride of the Balkans." He had won a match in the fourth round over Liaodong Turkic, "the Pride of Outer Mongolia."

I said, "Congratulations, Igor. It must feel good to win this match. It was a tough five sets."

He said, "Yes, to feel the winning is better for me than to feel the losingness that comes from the loss of not winning."

"You had good support from the crowd."

"Yes, I said to myself that the fans must support me if they have the sense of a jellyfish."

"I noticed you tended to glance at your coach in the box before the critical points. Were you receiving signals?"

"Yes, I must give credit to my coach. Also my dietician, my doctor, my chef, and my pilot."

"Was this the biggest win of your career?"

"Such questions are relative. Many things depend on the line calls of the idiots who are assigned by other idiots to judge important things."

"You were down two sets."

"Yes, the press will say this, but in my mind it was a different story, and this is for me to say when I have thought about it."

"Your serve brought you back."

"Yes, it is my style. To hit a high percentage of first serves and take away his serve by coming back low and to his feet."

"Doesn't everybody try to do that?"

"Yes, but the mental aspect must come into play with the mind."

"You've been quoted saying the key to winning at tennis is to keep the ball on the other side of the net. That's obvious, isn't it?"

"Yes. But it is not obvious unless you hit the ball there, *n'est-ce-pas?*"

"If you were to win this championship, how will you celebrate?"

"Yes. I have an expo in Sardinia that will pay me four million. After that, I will go to my villa in France and to my chalet in Switzerland. If there is time before my expo tour in Japan, I will buy a town and a diamond mine."

"We'll see you at the United States Open, right?"

"I am discussing this with my agent, lawyer, trainer, accountant, and fiancée. The Open in America has not agreed to change the dates to accommodate my busy schedule. Some people have no consideration for the athlete."

"I think we're done here," I said.

"Yes, it has been your privilege."

"Little Miss Poker Face"

SOME CALL IT A NUISANCE, even a curse, but I say it's fun to suffer waves of nostalgia for things I never knew.

Things like, you know, the Ottoman Empire, the Battle of Chicka-mauga, the Boer Wars, or, closer to home, the West Side Tennis Club at Forest Hills when it was host to the US National Tennis Championships for over sixty years.

Ah, Forest Hills. Sorry if you missed it. The grass courts, the trees, the hedges, the umbrella tables, the coziness, the charm, the Tudor clubhouse with its 416 gables.

I was there twice in the seventies—shortly before the US Nationals were kidnapped and taken to romantic Flushing in Queens. The last time I looked, it wasn't breaking a federal law to miss the quaint atmosphere of old sporting landmarks like Forest Hills. I would be equally saddened if cherished venues like the Rose Bowl, Wrigley Field, and Churchill Downs were discarded in the name of progress, or more likely to pad a developer's portfolio.

It's fine with me that the Billie Jean King National Tennis Center in Flushing has a stadium named for a trumpet player. Louis Armstrong did once live nearby, they say. I love Satchmo. His horn, his voice. I will forever listen to his recordings. I just never think of him playing a set of tennis against Harry James or Bunny Berigan.

But given the direction in which this modern center keeps expanding, and the direction in which our culture is spiraling downward, it won't surprise me if another stadium court is constructed and named for Garth Brooks rather than, say, Helen Wills Moody.

Ah, Helen.

It should never be forgotten that Helen Wills, who became Helen Wills Moody by marriage halfway through her career, was the diva of female sporting figures throughout the twenties and thirties as an amateur in an era when tennis was exclusively an amateur sport.

Young fans of the game deserve to know how talented Helen was and what an impact she had on the sport.

Helen was slender, attractive, regal in her bearing. She owned the grass courts at Forest Hills as solidly as she owned the grass courts at Wimbledon. She introduced the knee-length skirt and white visor to women's tennis. Along the way, she developed the attack of hitting the ball harder than any lady ever had.

At the top of her game she appeared on every significant magazine cover—twice on *Time* as well as on the *Saturday Evening Post, Vanity Fair, Tatler,* and the *Bystander,* the most popular sporting journal of her day.

Helen was more than a tennis champion. She was a graduate of the University of California at Berkeley, but that was long before the school became an annex of the Kremlin. She wrote poetry, magazine articles, and books, one of which was a mystery novel titled *Death Scores an Ace.* She painted well enough to be exhibited often. She posed for the artist Diego Rivera in his thirty-foot mural that hangs in the San Francisco Stock Exchange. She also posed for a marble bust, "Helen of California," which occupies a spot in the de Young Fine Arts Museum in Golden Gate Park.

For all of that, Helen Wills Moody may have achieved the pinnacle of stardom when Grantland Rice gave her the nickname, "Little Miss Poker Face." Rice had noted that Helen concentrated so deeply in matches she never changed expressions, win or lose a point.

Even Charlie Chaplin, America's premier entertainer in those days, was enamored of her. He was quoted saying, "The most beautiful movement I have ever seen is Helen Wills on a tennis court."

Helen said of herself, "The two things I loved best about tennis were hitting the ball hard and the rallies. I grew up loving any ball that bounced."

Which evidently eliminated polo, croquet, bowling, cricket, bocce, and the shot put from her life.

HER TENNIS RECORDS say more about her than anything else. Start with the fact that she still ranks fourth on the all-time list of singles victories in Grand Slam events. She won nineteen. Only Margaret Court with twenty-four, Serena Williams with twenty-three, and Steffi Graf with twenty-two are ahead of her.

But it should be mentioned that eleven of Margaret Court's twenty-four wins came in the Australian Open when nobody cared about it but Margaret and a couple of kangaroos. Helen never entered the Australian Open—it wasn't a Grand Slam event in her day. Thus she had one less major to compete for. All of her majors were won in the United States, England, and France.

If you match Helen's record against the other greats in only those three Grand Slam championships, you'll come up with a different list.

Helen Wills Moody—nineteen.

Steffi Graf—eighteen.

Chris Evert—sixteen.

Serena Williams—sixteen.

Little Miss Poker Face won seven US Nationals on the grass at Forest Hills. That might be the true record. A lady named Molla Mallory is credited with eight. But Mallory won her first four starting in 1915, shortly after Forest Hills opened, an era in which lady tennis players wore long dresses, wide-brimmed hats, and skipped about on the courts looking like they were trying to catch butterflies with their racquets.

During Helen's reign as the queen of tennis, she won eight Wimbledon singles titles—*eight*—her last coming in 1939. Those eight lasted as the record for over fifty years, until Martina Navratilova won her ninth at Wimbledon in 1990.

Helen added four French national titles to her list of majors. And it's a nice footnote that she won the gold medal in both singles and doubles—with Hazel Wightman as a partner—in the 1924 Summer Olympics in Paris.

THEY SAY IT'S IMPOSSIBLE to compare athletes from different eras, but if you want to know what I think would happen if Helen Wills Moody and Serena Williams faced one another at the peak of their talents, I'll share my personal opinion with you.

Put them on the grass courts of old Forest Hills and let them play a series of battles using today's balls and racquets—or the equipment of Helen's day, either one—and Little Miss Poker Face will wind up with all of Serena Williams's trophies and Maria Sharapova's endorsements.

Winter Wonders

ALL ANYONE KNEW about winter sports for years was that a little blond dish named Sonja Henie toddled out of Norway to steal our hearts—and occasionally Adolf Hitler's, if you believed the gossip columnists—by regularly winning the gold medal in figure skating at the Winter Olympics.

Sonja took gold at St. Moritz in 1928, at Lake Placid in 1932, and at Garmisch-Partenkirchen in 1936. After which, it's been said that she tried to kill the Winter Olympics by becoming a movie star in the United States.

There was one thing you could count on when you watched a Sonja Henie movie. She might be a shopgirl, a maid, an inkeeper's daughter, even a spy, but somewhere in the plot she would happen upon a frozen pond.

A pair of ice skates would attach themselves to her dainty feet, accordion music would come out of somewhere, and in her platinum hair worn like a skullcap Sonja would go gliding and hopping over the ice.

I used to contend that the best thing about the Winter Olympics was that it disappeared for four years at a time. Like somebody once said, figure skating's not a sport, it's dinner theater. I wish I'd thought of that.

But lately the figure skaters have gone from landing triple jumps to nailing quads and I've had to re-think my position. These people are super athletes.

Then there's speed skating, a totally different thing. There are 713 speed skating events in the Winter Games. This is a sport where people wear yoga pants and helmets, swing only one arm as they skate around an oval, and don't stop until their thighs explode.

Most of the men's races are won by Rutger, the Axe of Amsterdam. The women's division is dominated by Hilda, the Beast of Bavaria.

Cross-country ski racing would confuse Harvard. It appears there *is* an event in progress, but there are so many entrants trekking in and out of the woods it's hard to know whether the competition is starting or ending. The winner may well be a Norwegian spectator who wasn't even entered.

Bobsledding has its loyal followers. Here's a sport in which demented people sit in a sled that goes two thousand miles an hour in an ice tunnel with sharp curves. This is almost as terrifying to watch as the luge (feet first) or the skeleton (headfirst) where the athlete, male or female, lies down on a cafeteria tray and goes through ice tunnels at five thousand miles an hour.

Nordic ski jumping attracts every lunatic who is not a bobsledder. The athlete zooms down the world's tallest slide and sails into the air headfirst, hoping to land somewhere near his home country.

Beneath him, fifty thousand people eagerly await his arrival, knowing that three things can happen. He will win, he will be paralyzed for life, he will die.

The least watched event in the Winter Olympics is the biathlon. This is because the sport is so misunderstood. But there is nothing complicated about the biathlon. A Russian puts on a pair of skis, picks up a rifle, roams around in a forest, and stops every once in a while to shoot a German.

Alpine ski racing has long held its place as the glamour event of winter, thanks to athletes who like sliding down a hill at ninety miles an hour, laugh at turning cartwheels for two hundred yards, become adept at veering off course at sharp turns and winding up in St. Anton when he or she was hoping to go to Gstaad, and tolerate having one leg in a cast for three months out of every year.

Today, however, the sport is under attack from snowboarders and a different brand of skier. They turn endless flips, twists, and sky walks in midair doing halfpipes, stove lids, and can openers, and frequently ski on the tops of fence rails, hardly ever getting killed in any of these acts. On boards or skis, they do things only a teenager or an escaped convict would attempt.

They will continue to gain popularity when they learn to say something other than, "I'm just gonna lay one down and see what happens."

I still prefer the places where covering Alpine ski racing took me. Kitzbuhel, Wengen, Zermatt, and Val-d'Isere suited me nicely. And the

French and Austrian racers, I hear from colleagues, still give the most intriguing interviews.

The Frenchman says:

"I come from Saint-le-Chemise, you have been? A skier only has two legs at the top. Yes, more wine. You are paying? I must have that woman over there. Is she rich?"

The Austrian says:

"My home is Kleiner Sterner. It is beautiful, you have been? Yes, I lost the downhill at Swine-Plotz. Sometimes the slopes do not go with my skis. Here, I must win, but the mountain will tell my feet. One day when I retire I will move back home and take a bath."

The sport Sonja Henie invented might make the most sense, after all. It's indoors, it's warm, it's dramatic, and it's always suspenseful as to what the Russian judges might do.

In the women's division you can score the best set of wheels on the babes, and with the men you get to see a bunch of guys dressed like Robin Hood.

Man Your Umlauts

IN AN EARLIER STAGE of my development I spent nine winters covering Alpine ski racing on the slopes of Europe, which largely consisted of watching men and women schuss from Alp to Alp while I schussed from raclette to fondue and back again. There were worse jobs.

During one of those years it dawned on me that the perfect war would match the Swiss against the Swedes. Neither country had been in a war for seven thousand years. It was time they got roughed up.

If they fired enough umlauts and hyphens at each other, we could rid the world of many of the dullest people in it. Of course the Swiss and Swedes can't help it if they're dull. It has to do with geography.

Sweden is off over there somewhere near some fjords, though not as many fjords as Norway has, if you insist on accuracy in the matter. On the other hand, if you've seen one fjord, you've seen them all.

There have never been more than twenty-seven people in Sweden at a time, except for a moment during World War II when assorted German field marshals were in and out of Stockholm on business and pleasure.

Ten of the twenty-seven Swedes refuse to speak at all. This has to do with their climate. They live in darkness four months of the year and when the sun does come out it never rises above their heads. Cloudy is popular in Sweden.

Of the seventeen other Swedes, nine of them are actresses named Ingrid, four are men named Lars who write books about tattooed girls with guns who like to get even with bad guys, and four are jovial businessmen named Sven who laugh at things no one of sound mind would find humorous.

I once had the privilege of dining with a jovial Sven. Between courses, he broke an armchair and one window pane although I don't recall him saying anything other than, "Ha-ho-ha! Goot! Hot tub! Fish! Love! More glogg!"

IF IT ONLY SEEMS that the Swiss are more interesting than the Swedes, it's because of their terrain. In the Alps a Swiss person is always leaning in one direction or another.

There are no more Swiss than there are Swedes. The same twenty-seven in all. Everyone else in Switzerland is a tourist.

But it's a mistake to believe that half the people in Switzerland speak French and the other half speak German. Every Swiss person speaks three languages—wrist watch, chocolate, numbered account.

I have this recurring dream of my wife and I combining a vacation with my work and we're lost in the Alps. We can't find the cozy chalet we've rented. I approach a Swiss gentleman in a village that's cozy but not ours.

"Excuse me," I say. "Can you help us get back to Fondue-sur-le-Steep?"

He says, "Chocolate?"

"No thank you," I say.

"Wrist watch?"

"Not really interested, but thanks."

"Numbered account?"

"Another time, maybe. I'm trying to find the chalet we've rented. I know it's near here. The town is not big. It sits on a ledge. There's a steeple in the village. Quite a bit of neatly stacked firewood in places."

He pointed to the top of the Jungfrau.

"It's up there?" I said, gaping.

"No. Fondue-sur-le-Steep is down below us. But you must go up there to get down here. It is the way of the mountains."

"Maybe I should call a taxi," I said.

"There are no taxis. The roads are too dangerous."

"What about a train? I'll leave our rent car here."

"Many trains, yes. They come every hour, but you must be alert to jump on board. There! You just missed one down the hill."

"I see," I said. "What if I pay you to drive us? This is your car here?"

"This is not a car."

"What is it?"

"My Rolex. I'm polishing it."

"But it has wheels, and room for three. How much would you charge?"

"That would be . . . let's see . . ."

He yodels as he removes a pocket calculator from his lederhosen.

". . . it would come to . . . in American . . . counting the quart of milk I will need for nourishment on the return trip . . . one thousand two hundred and eighty-two dollars and . . . and twenty-seven cents."

"Deal," I say, as the dream ends. "Fill it up with unleaded chocolate and we're outta here."

Summer Sensations

A TENSE MOMENT in every Summer Olympics is when the captivating teenage gymnast has the weight of an entire nation riding on her backward triple flip on the balance beam. Will she continue to be the charming coquette of the Games or turn into a choking midget?

Since the beam is only four inches wide, merely thinking about the event makes my crotch hurt. The dreaded beam should be banned from all gymnastic competitions—these children are asked to achieve something only my Yorkshire terrier can do.

It's not surprising that the hottest ticket at the Summer Olympics is for women's gymnastics, as the tickets least in demand are for Greco-Roman grunting. Dirty old men in raincoats stand in line for months ahead to buy them.

Of course half of the tickets are purchased by the mothers of the charming coquettes, all of whom have been trained since birth to seek gold medals and wind up on Wheaties boxes, which will put them in a position to support their parents.

I deny the existence of men's gymnastics. The floor exercises alone resemble tryouts for a hip-hop musical on Broadway that I would only attend if I were bound in wire and dragged by members of the Aryan Brotherhood.

And those rings the guys do things on?

Only an orangutan is fit for that.

Estimates have it that the ancient Olympics began between the eighth century BC and the fourth century AD, and the athletes competed in an array of events that included Hurling the Slave, Stabbing the Lion, Lifting the Rock, and Wrecking the Chariot.

The modern Olympics, the one we watch now, started in 1896 in Athens. It happened to include the three sports that are popular in the Games of today.

Swimming, gymnastics, track and field.

However, this was back when the young men and women had trouble swimming faster than barracudas. The male swimmers were required to wear shirts and shorts and the ladies were required to wear burlap gowns.

Today Olympic swimmers set a world record in every race, partly because of advances in swimwear. They are fitted in skin suits, skin caps, and tiny goggles which help them slice through the pool much faster.

Maybe the barracudas should be allowed to wear skin suits, skin caps, and tiny goggles so they can keep up with the USA's teenage girls.

AS FOR TRACK AND FIELD, Jesse Owens owned it. Jesse and the four gold medals he won at the Berlin Olympics in '36. He won the 100 dash, the 200 dash, the long jump, and was part of the victorious 4x100 relay, all of which is said to have given Hitler an ulcer.

It's widely held that Jesse Owens was the only American black man in the '36 Olympics as well as the only American black man who had ever competed in an Olympics.

Not so.

At the '32 Olympics in Los Angeles, four years earlier, two American black athletes, Eddie Tolan and Ralph Metcalfe, dominated the dashes. Tolan and Metcalfe ran 1-2 in the 100, and Tolan won the 200, Metcalfe finishing third. This was the same Ralph Metcalfe who joined Jesse Owens, Foy Draper, and Frank Wykoff on the 4x100 relay team in Berlin. Pause for historical correction. America thus had two black athletes to give the Führer his ulcer.

If you've never seen the film of that relay final you have a right to assume that Jesse ran anchor for the USA, him being the fastest of the four. But in fact he ran the opening leg, Metcalfe ran second, Foy Draper third, and Frank Wykoff anchored, as he had on winning the 4x100 relay in '32.

One might wonder how much faster Owens could have run if he'd worn today's lightweight sneakers with ceramic spikes and competed on today's synthetic rubberized surfaces as opposed to the leather shoes with metal spikes he wore while sprinting on the crunchy cinders of his era.

Some forty years after his Berlin heroics, I went to see *Songbook*, a hit musical comedy on the London stage. It dealt with a fictitious songwriter named "Mooney Shapiro" who endeavored to write hit songs through the decades but kept turning out hilarious flops.

Among many of the show-stopping numbers was one about Jesse Owens and the '36 Olympic Games. Here is one verse that was performed by "Mooney," who appeared dressed as the Führer.

All my trouble vas beginning
when the schwartza started winning.
You're a Nazi Party Pooper, Jesse O.
Fame never leaves certain athletes.

The First World's
Fastest Human

WHEN THE ANCIENT OLYMPIC GAMES started in Olympia, Greece, it was accepted by everyone that the winner of the 100-cobblestone dash would be crowned the world's fastest human. It's incidental that the athlete covered the distance in an estimated twenty-seven minutes with a spear in his back.

The winner of that race is not listed in available records, but it's rumored that his toga came from Under Armour and his sandals from Nike. No one knows who threw the spear, only that it was purchased from Apollo's Sporting Goods.

Over time a host of world's fastest humans have presented themselves to us. The best known are Charley Paddock in the twenties, Jesse Owens in the thirties, Mel Patton in the forties, Bobby Morrow in the fifties, Bob Hayes in the sixties, Valery Borzov in the seventies, Carl Lewis in the eighties *and* nineties, and Usain Bolt in the millennium, unless you feel that Usain should be disqualified since he arrived from another galaxy.

Those sprinters could outrun a bullet train and any human of their day. But none of them can lay claim to having been the *original* world's fastest human. I was hoping you would ask who that was.

He was Howard P. Drew.

This young man held that title in the minds of sports fans and in the headlines of newspapers from 1912 through 1916 despite the fact that he never won an Olympic gold.

Drew was a young black kid born in Lexington, Virginia, and raised in Springfield, Massachusetts. While in high school, he won the 100-meter dash in the Olympic Trials, tying the existing world record of 10.5. It earned him a spot on the United States track team that sailed to Stockholm for the 1912 Summer Olympics.

The Stockholm Olympics are best remembered for Jim Thorpe's fantastic performance. That's where the legendary Carlisle footballer won gold medals in the decathlon *and* the pentathlon. Thorpe captured nine of the fifteen individual events in the two competitions and received the admiration of Sweden's King Gustav V, who said to Thorpe, "You, sir, are the world's greatest athlete."

Thorpe famously replied, "Thanks, king."

Excuse the segue.

Howard Drew could have left Stockholm with the same amount of glory had it not been for an injury. He was an overwhelming favorite to win the 100 and 200 dashes. In the 100 prelims he was leaving everybody so far behind they could only reach him by mail. But in the semifinals with a big lead near the finish, he pulled a muscle when he stepped on a soft spot in the cinders. He hobbled to the finish and won handily.

It's said that the stop watches had him on course to set a new world record. But the damage was done. The USA doctors held him out of both Olympic events out of fear that if he reinjured himself, his racing career would be over.

But Drew did race again—and faster. The University of Southern California took a chance on him, and he repaid the school with interest. Flying the Trojan colors, Drew in 1914 set a world record in the 100 with a 9.6 and another world record in the 200 with a 21.2. Both records were approved by the US Amateur Athletic Union.

By then he was already the favorite to sweep the dashes in the 1916 Olympics that were scheduled for Berlin. But once again Drew was a victim of bad timing. Those Summer Olympics were cancelled due to the slight inconvenience of World War I.

He had to be content with winning other competitions. One was at major track meets held at Pasadena's Tournament Park, which at the time was where the early Rose Bowl football games were played.

It was also in 1916 that a bizarre event was staged on the outskirts of Paris. Precisely at a time when things weren't exactly all quiet on the Western Front, and before the United States entered the war, our government sent one hundred athletes to Paris to compete in what was called

"The Pershing Olympics." The competition involved twenty-two Allied nations. Howard P. Drew dominated the sprints.

Here was a guy who would have won four Olympic gold medals in the dashes were it not for the combination of a freak injury and poor timing in his track career. He was left to devote the rest of his life to that of a soldier who became a scholar, lawyer, and judge.

Not bad, as consolation prizes go, for the original world's fastest human.

To Break a Barrier

THE MILE RUN in the sport of track and field is the only distance race that doesn't strike Americans as silly. The mile is the glamor race. Who would run ten thousand meters for any reason? I mean, other than an Ethiopian or a Kenyan looking for a convenience store?

Ever since America's Glenn Cunningham, "the Kansas Flyer," set the mile record of 4:06.8 in 1934 and kept it for three years, which must have seemed longer during the Depression, we have held the mile run in the same thing as awe.

The mile makes sense.

A man will run a mile to grab a taxi in Manhattan.

A man will run a mile to reach a football stadium before the kickoff.

A man will run a mile to avoid a TV set that's showing the Kardashians.

Glenn Cunningham was the ultimate miler in the minds of America's sports fans until World War II. While that conflict was going on, good old neutral Sweden produced a runner named Gunder Hägg. Gunder sliced away at the mile record from '42 through '45 by racing in the safety of Gothenburg, Stockholm, and Malmo and gradually lowered the mark from 4:06.3 to 4:01.4. By that time, Americans were pronouncing his name properly—Hahg, as in eggnog.

The mile run's four-minute barrier stayed unattainable for nine more years, but there came a day in 1954 that lives on in the memory of cindermen, distancemen, tracksters, and owners of stopwatches everywhere.

Today's youth may not recognize the name of Roger Bannister, believing as it does that the history of anything involving sports, politics, war, culture, and show biz begins with their birth.

Isn't Pearl Harbor that resort in the Caribbean? I know I've seen TV commercials for it.

Dr. Roger Bannister, Englishman, neurologist, and consummate amateur, broke the barrier on May 6, 1954, in a race at Oxford where he was clocked in 3:59.4. Screaming front page headlines notified the world of it. The news was stupefying to most people. It was like finding out halfway through your life that New Hampshire has a coastline.

But Bannister's feat was only the beginning of the assault. Now that he had plundered the psychological wall of four minutes, distance runners everywhere joined in.

Six weeks later, on June 21, the Australian runner, John Landy, in a race in Turku, Finland, posted a time of 3:58.0. Now two men had cracked the barrier. And when it was learned that a month and a half later Bannister and Landy would clash in the mile run at the British Empire and Commonwealth Games in Vancouver, the sports world flipped out.

Overnight the upcoming race began to be hailed as "The Miracle Mile," "The Dream Mile," and "The Race of the Century."

Sports Illustrated was fortunate that the race took place in time for its inaugural issue, which came on August 16, 1954. Paul O'Neil, one of *Time* magazine's finest writers, covered the race for *SI*, and his brilliant piece begins:

"The art of running the mile consists, in essence, of reaching the threshold of unconsciousness at the instant of breasting the tape."

Landy was aware of Bannister's habit of saving himself for a late kick in the home stretch, so the Australian's plan was to go out front early and set a torrid pace that would force Bannister to keep up with him and wear down. This would deprive Roger of his closing burst.

Landy did exactly that. On the back stretch of the first lap Landy left the pack of Bannister and six other runners behind. He opened a gap of fifteen yards between himself and Bannister.

On the second lap Bannister himself left the pack, but he still trailed Landy by twelve to fifteen yards. He slowly moved up on Landy in the third lap, closing the distance to five yards. When the split time was announced, the crowd was on its feet, roaring and clapping, knowing that both men were on schedule to break four minutes.

Into the last seventy-five yards the two milers headed home with Bannister on Landy's right shoulder, a stride or two behind. It was over the last fifty yards that Landy felt certain Bannister had nothing left. But a telling photo shows Landy glancing to his left to see precisely where

Roger was just as Bannister explodes past him on the outside. From there, Bannister literally flies to the tape and finishes three yards ahead of Landy and collapses into the arms of his trainer—and hordes of track officials, photographers, and writers.

Roger Bannister had run the mile in 3:58.9, John Landy in 3:59.6.

It was indeed the race of a lifetime, and it hasn't been equaled since.

In the years that followed I've listened to sports scribes older and wiser than myself discuss "the athletic heart," or whatever it is that gives an athlete in any sport the will to win, no matter the cost, and propels him to victory. The majority of them determined that Roger Bannister, first by breaking the four-minute mile, and then by defeating John Landy in their duel, had twice proved to have the greatest heart of any athlete they'd seen or studied. His will to win was unmatched.

I agree. Since 1954 the world record for the mile has been gradually lowered a total of eighteen seconds by twelve different runners, including the United Kingdom's fab trio of Sebastian Coe, Steve Ovett, and Steve Cram, who tossed the record back and forth between them throughout the eighties.

The mile record at this moment of typing is 3:43.13. It was set by Morocco's Hicham El Guerrouj on July 7, 1999, in a race in Rome. That was eighteen years ago.

But there was no Roger Bannister in that race. Had there been, I think I know what would have happened.

Bannister would have run a 3:43.12.

Champ for the Ages

THANKS TO ELECTRICAL WONDERS, I have been able to watch and re-watch many of the famous sporting events in history, including one of the great prizefights of the century—Joe Louis against Billy Conn for the heavyweight championship of the world in 1941. When I listened to the fight live on the radio as an excited youngster, it left me agog, if not more so.

The bout took place on the night of June 18 of that year, "outdoors in the ballpark," as Marlon Brando would say, in New York's Polo Grounds before a crowd of 54,487 customers.

This was the long-awaited collision in which the flashy young Billy Conn made the unbeatable Joe Louis look alarmingly beatable for twelve smart rounds by stinging Louis with combinations while dancing, ducking, weaving, and staying out of Joe's knockout range.

But in the thirteenth round, the brash Billy Conn, although safely ahead on points, switched his style. He tried to slug it out with Louis—and lost. Concealed in Louis's right glove was an iron fist, and that punch kept Joe the heavyweight champion for what came to be known as the "Duration," a term applied to the length of time it was going to take the Greatest Generation to win World War II.

That fight remains a classic, one of the ten greatest in the history of human mayhem. The film lives up to the drama of the radio broadcast, which in itself is a rare thing, I can tell you from experience.

That fight was the last heavyweight championship bout that meant anything around my house. I happen to be a person who never saw Rocky Marciano do anything but maul a guy into a sack of feed in a corner, and I am someone who never saw Muhammed Ali actually *hit* anybody very hard. I'm certain that Ali never hit Sonny Liston at all that time Liston went down in the first round. I did see Joe Frazier hit Ali solidly a considerable number of times. I had a good seat at the first Ali-Frazier fight in Madison Square Garden.

In contrast, Joe Louis would noticeably hit people, often knocking them down, and usually out. I frequently watched him accomplish that in the newsreels.

Louis even survived his familiar introductions by the ring announcers, which went: "And in this corner, standing six foot one, weighing 207 pounds, 'the Brown Bomber,' always a credit to his race, the heavyweight champion of the world, Joe Louis!"

If a ring announcer spouted those words today, he would be ripped to shreds by a gang of politically correct minions before the fight started.

In his later years Louis exhibited a sense of humor. It was on a cable TV show in New York with Ali when Ali was holding the heavyweight crown and asked Joe how he thought he would do against him, "the greatest."

Louis tried to avoid the question, saying they fought in different eras, had different styles. Joe mentioned that he'd once fought a series of bouts against heavyweights that sportswriters dubbed "the Bum of the Month Tour." In order of their becoming intimate with the canvas, the tour consisted of Al McCoy, Red Burman, Gus Dorazio, Abe Simon, Tony Musto, and Buddy Baer.

"You calling me a bum?" Ali said.

"I didn't say that," Joe said.

"Yes, you did," Ali raged. "You implied it."

Grinning, Joe said, "You'd have been on the tour."

Louis's fight with Billy Conn in '41 was all the more memorable in that it was the closest Louis came to defeat in his prime.

Billy Conn had boyish good looks and was a clever, stylish fighter with a decent punch of his own. The trouble was, he gave away reach, height, and twenty-five pounds to Louis. Yet on that night he had the champion confused and tagged him repeatedly. Conn might well have taken the title if he hadn't grown overconfident.

In the film of the fight it's surprising to watch how skillfully Conn scored points and kept out of Joe's reach, particularly in the third, fourth, seventh, ninth, eleventh, and twelfth rounds. Not known as a knockout artist, Conn clearly staggers Louis twice with his jarring combinations, a fierce left jab being his most effective weapon.

Even in the eventful thirteenth round, Conn was holding his own as he traded blows with Louis. But with only twelve seconds left in the round, and as they came out of a clinch, Louis suddenly caught Billy with a right uppercut, a left hook, and—the knockout punch—a jolting right to the jaw.

Conn went down, but he wasn't out cold. He dizzily tried to rise before Referee Eddie Joseph reached the count of ten—but failed.

ONE NIGHT many years ago in Pittsburgh I met Billy Conn. It was through a mutual friend, and the three of us made a tour of Conn's favorite hangouts.

We started at the exclusive Duquesne Club where Billy knew a member. From there we hit places Conn referred to as the Bachelor's Club, the Suffering Mothers Club, and a place simply known as The Bar. We looked in on Birdie's Hurricane and The Grill, two popular joints in town where black folks and white folks mingled convivially to drink, dine, and enjoy the jazz artists who performed there.

Billy confessed that the toughest fight he ever had wasn't with Joe Louis but a few years earlier when he won a split decision over Fritzie Zivic, another Pittsburgh battler.

Conn said, "Fritzie was tough and quick. He could catch a fly by the wings with his thumb and forefinger. I seen it happen for my own money. Fritzie was the dirtiest fighter who ever stepped in a ring. He tried to gouge my eyes out."

Billy reminded me that he and Zivic were both world champions.

"That's something, huh?" he said. "A mick and a hunky from Pittsburgh holding titles at the same time. Him in the welters, me in the light heavies."

The mutual friend urged Billy to tell me about the time he matched himself against some mob guys.

Billy said. "I got in on a legit deal with 'em, but I come up on the short end. They stiffed me. They hung out in this hotel suite I knew about, so I decided to go get what was coming to me. Only time in my life I ever carried a gun. I busted in on 'em, pulled out the gun, and said, "I'm Billy Conn and I'm here to get my money from you bums."

Like a standup comic, Billy paused long enough in his narrative for me to ask, "What happened?"

"I got laughed at," he said.

When he got around to talking about the fight with Joe Louis, he said, "The Pittsburgh Irish come out in me. I knew I had him beat, but I wanted to knock him out. But even if I'd won on points and took the belt with me when I joined the Army, Joe still would have made my life hell for four years."

I said. "Why was that?"

Billy said, "Knowing when the war was over I was gonna have to fight the son of a bitch again."

The Search

A CASE CAN BE MADE that the sport of prizefighting lost considerable interest in this country when we ran out of oppressed minorities.

There's no need to bother looking among heavyweights in America to find the next Great White Hope, or even the next Great Diversified Hope. Today you won't find more than one American titleholder in the other weights, including the light cruiser middle welterweight division, which didn't exist until a moment ago.

Last time I looked, the world champs in every category currently came from Mexico, Japan, the Philippines, United Kingdom, Kazakhstan, Ukraine, Venezuela, Russia, and Cuba. Our oppressed minorities clearly aren't what they used to be.

Throughout the thirties, forties, and fifties there were many years when American prizefighters held every title—and outpunched other Americans to win those titles.

But this was when the young men among our oppressed minorities couldn't find work in a mill, mine, plant, or factory unless they knew Lee J. Cobb.

They were left with the choice of joining up with Meyer Lansky, or sitting on the front stoops of buildings smoking cigarettes, or looking for the rich kid in the neighborhood so they could beat him up for getting ball-bearing skates and a bike for his birthday.

The inquisitive found a gym.

In short, we don't produce guys who like to be hit in the face anymore. They have welfare. I remember when prizefighters looked like they liked being hit in the face. They had the bent noses and swollen cheeks to show for it.

Any list of these tigers would include Fritzie Zivic, of course, along with Barney Ross, Willie Pep, Lou Ambers, Rocky Graziano, Tony Zale, Henry Armstrong, Beau Jack, Carmen Basilio, Kid Gavilan, and, although he seldom got hit, Sugar Ray Robinson, pound for pound the greatest prizefighter who ever lived. The smartest boxing authorities I know agree on this.

Not to overlook Jake LaMotta, about whom you have to say the saloons of America became a safer place after Jake reached old age. Incidentally, Jake never looked like Robert De Niro in the first place. The Jake LaMotta that I watched terrorize people in Manhattan bars was the size of *two* Robert De Niros.

THIS IS ONLY A GUESS, but if you were to find a mill, mine, plant, or factory anywhere in this country today, you probably wouldn't see scores of workers lifting things, fitting things, tightening things, and becoming so angry by the end of the day that they wouldn't go home until they enjoyed a good fist fight on a sidewalk. They have it better now.

You might see a group of employees relaxing, reading paperbacks or Kindles, and pausing every so often to push a button and let a machine do the work. Then it would be time for lunch.

Full disclosure: I've been involved in only two fights in my life. One was with the ribbon reverse on an Olivetti portable. The other was with a desktop Dell that swallowed three chapters of a novel in progress. I lost both conflicts.

Timing had it that I came along too late to cover three legendary fight managers, Mike Jacobs, Al Weill, and George Gainford. They handled Joe Louis, Rocky Marciano, and Sugar Ray Robinson, respectively.

But I did have an old high school friend, Scott Sherman, who dabbled in the sport as a hobby. He had been the early trainer of Paulie Ayala, a Fort Worth kid, and he'd had something to do with handling Paulie when the kid fought his way to the world bantamweight championship.

One day while chatting with Scott about the fight business—more like joking around—I said people didn't seem to care about the sport as much as they once did.

Scott said, "The fight game's not over in this country—it's just in a lull. If it goes on too long, Vegas will invent somebody."

I said, "Have you seen any prospects in the gyms?"

"What gyms?" he said. "It's all health clubs now."

I said, "Yeah, I've looked in one of those. All I saw were people pedaling stationary bikes while they watched the Food Channel on TV."

Scott said, "How long since you've seen a fist fight in a street? Not since high school or college, right?"

I said, "I could probably find one if I stood around long enough in the parking lot of a honky tonk in West Texas."

Scott said, "There aren't any more street fights. Today if a street punk has a disagreement with another street punk, or anybody else, he'll just pull out a gun and shoot him. It's quicker."

Going Flat-Out

SOMEBODY COULD POUR a bucket of grease on my head and you still wouldn't confuse me for an authority on automobile racing. Even in my advancing years I'm unable to tell the difference between a head gasket and a camshaft, or an Offenhauser from a Penske, much less keep all the Unsers straight in my mind.

What I will tell you is that I've been a fan of the Indy 500 since my kid days. It was a time when I listened attentively to the race on the radio every Memorial Day and rooted for Lou Meyer to beat Rex Mays to the finish at the breakneck speed of ninety-nine miles an hour.

A week later I would look forward to the afternoon when a member of the family would take me to a movie theater and I'd watch highlights of the Indy 500, courtesy of Pathé News, Fox Movietone News, or Paramount News. That would precede the feature film, which would star George Brent conducting business in three-piece suits.

I would be excited to watch the same daredevils, Lou Meyer and Rex Mays, speed around the "brickyard" in their open-cockpit Stutz Bearcats, which soon enough would begin to look less like Stutz Bearcats than they did Grumman Hellcats and Curtiss P-40 Warhawks with their wings sawed off.

What I *did* know was that the Indy 500 was—and still is—the only auto race that means anything, just as the Olympics is the only track meet, Elvis is the only rock star, Sinatra is the only crooner, Frankenstein is the only monster, Ava Gardner is the only temptress, and Lassie is the only dog.

I ATTENDED THE INDY 500 ONCE. It was in 1961, the year A. J. Foyt won it for the first time. My biggest surprise was that I could only see part of the track from my area of the press box—the straightway start and finish. The reason I knew the race was over was because this guy up on a tower waved a black-and-white checkered flag that I knew about from the newsreels.

I well remember the noise, smell, crashes, confusion, and the 400,000 fans that made the infield look like mall shoppers on the day after Thanksgiving.

I hadn't realized how far the two-and-a-half mile track stretched. Out of sight is where it went. Other than the race drivers, I'm not sure anyone had seen a whole Indy 500 until it began to be televised in the sixties.

A LITTLE HISTORY. In the beginning, which was in 1909, the track was constructed of crushed rocks and dirt, but it was rapidly done over in red bricks—hence the nickname of "brickyard." Through the years of wear and tear, the bricks began to require asphalt patchwork in spots. It was before the 1962 Indy that the track was totally resurfaced with asphalt, which helped increase the speeds. That and the coming of the rear engine, or so I've been told.

There is one yard of the old red bricks left. It marks the start-finish line. It's become a ritual for the winner to kneel and "kiss the bricks" after he's drowned himself with the traditional bottle of sweet milk.

It goes without saying that I remember how loud the race is. For noise, the Indy 500 can hold its own against any deranged pop, rock, or country concert.

The year I was there A. J. Foyt won with an average speed of 139 miles an hour. A big leap from the thirties, but nothing compared to what has followed.

Winning speeds have steadily increased to the point where in 2013 a fellow named Tony Kanaan from Brazil behind the wheel and in front of a Chevy engine, not to ignore the aid of his heavy right foot, won with an average speed of 187.4 miles an hour.

Think about that. A guy drives in traffic for 500 miles at speeds that used to apply to airplanes.

One thing I've given up trying to pin down is how Jim Nabors got the ceremonial job of singing "Back Home in Indiana" all those years to help start every car's engine. Jim wasn't a native of Indiana. He was from Alabama.

I gather he must have once seen moonlight on the Wabash as he looked down from his window seat in an American Airlines jet while traveling from LA to Indianapolis.

Research in another area tells me that the Offenhauser holds the record for the most Indy wins for an engine with twenty-seven. That's almost as many as the Unsers have won by driving their Stutz Bearcats powered by Offys, Fords, Cosworths, Chevies, Penskes, and Mercedes-Benz engines.

I speak of the victorious Unsers with whom Indy 500 fans have become so familiar—Al Unser, Bobby Unser, Al Unser Jr., Parnelli Unser, Mario Unser, Rick Unser, Helio Unser, and Dario Unser.

That may not be all of them. Correct me if I've overlooked any others.

The Car Groupie

MAXINE HUBBARD'S website was irresistible. She presents herself as a one-time housewife, good mother, and a super car-racing groupie. She loves the movie that's been made of her life and she's happy with the title the studio settled on after a deluge of bitter discussions: *My Life Was the Pits*.

She says on the site, "It's the story of a woman who devotes two marriages and half her life to auto racing and don't come away with nothing to show for it but heartache. I would have enjoyed the movie even if it was about some other woman, although not as much."

Maxine adds, "I hope Crystal Clay wins some of the big awards for her work in this movie. She should have won the Oscar two years ago for *Revenge*, the flick where she plays a female bank robber who becomes a United States Senator. I do wish they hadn't made her a brunette doing me."

HOW COULD I MISS attending the first stop on Maxine's publicity tour? It was held at Junior's 24-Hour Café and Quick Lube on Farm Road 16 in Georgia next door to Ginger's All-Day Breakfast, Guns, and Knitwear.

I had trouble finding it, but I arrived in time to watch Maxine stride to the microphone with a longneck Bud in her hand to welcome everybody. She did this while an irritable waitress in a ball cap and high-top tennis shoes passed out DVDs of the movie.

I estimated Maxine to be somewhere in her forties. She was trim and attractive if you didn't mind too much makeup and crinkly blond hair.

She started off thanking the studio, Filmwood, for setting up the tour. She admitted it was pure luck that she'd met the producer, Freddie Drake, when he was prowling around the pits during Indy qualifying. He liked the idea when Maxine suggested her life story would make a good movie. The producer became more interested in the idea later on in her motel room, she said, where they discussed the project in more detail.

Maxine hopes the movie will set the record straight about the lies, rumors, and innuendo in her life.

"Lisa Ann Grimes is responsible for spreading every rumor," Maxine said. "Lisa Ann told everybody in the trailer park and around the tracks that Joe Ed and me was getting it on while I was living with Shorty. Among other things, that wasn't fair to my husband Harley."

A writer asked if she would tell us a little more about the real Lisa Ann in real life. Not the one in the movie.

Maxine said, "She won't be showing her face around Darlington or Talladega anytime soon, or Daytona and Indy. It's in the movie about her sleeping around with Royce Henry and E. T. Brunson. Nobody's man was safe when that woman was on the loose. I've never understood why some men go for women just because they're top-heavy and talk dirty."

"It's not that big a mystery," a writer said, and got a laugh.

Smiling, Maxine said, "And I thought you looked like a leg man."

A louder laugh shook the room.

"Lisa Ann ain't worth talking about," Maxine said. "Anita Fraser who plays her in the movie makes her out to be more likable than she is, and even better looking if you want my opinion. There was always gossip about Lisa Ann in the pits. When you could hear, I should say."

Maxine, who has reclaimed her maiden name of Hubbard, confessed that her interest in car racing dated back to when she was growing up in Hollow Row, Iowa, and was constantly exposed to the horses and buggies that brought the Amish folks to town from their communities. She said, "If a horse and buggy won't get a girl interested in cars, I don't know what will."

She'd been a movie fan all her life. Especially the old black-and-white movies, the kind where Bette Davis chain-smoked cigarettes and gave everybody a hard time. She particularly recalled the convertible Bette Davis drove with the top down in one old movie. It had a title like *Is This Her Life or Somebody Else's*.

Maxine remembered how Bette Davis drove around recklessly in the convertible and finally got killed doing it, but the character deserved to die, being a spoiled society brat.

Maxine learned to drive when she was fifteen. Her daddy taught her in his Jeep Pickup. She said, "I liked letting those horses and buggies eat my dust. I don't know why everybody's not interested in cars. Cars are what people do."

A writer asked what it was that she liked best about car racing. Was it open wheel, closed wheel, Formula One, dirt track, midget auto, Kart, what?

Maxine said, "I like all of it. Of course there's nothing to compare with Indy and Daytona. But in every category the men are men, if you get my meaning. You don't hear a lot of talk about antique furniture."

That brought another laugh from the crowd.

Maxine said she mainly liked the action in the pits. "Anybody can push the pedal to the mat. Races are won in the pits."

That's why she dumped Harley to marry Joe Ed. She never gave a thought to marrying Shorty. He was only a hobby and the best jack-man on the circuit. Joe Ed Gibson was a man with a future.

Joe Ed was the crew chief for E. T. Brunson's team, and he was always looking for an edge. He invented shaving the letters off the side of a tire to reduce wind resistance.

Maxine said, "A pit man can be trouble, if you want the truth. Your pit man devotes a considerable amount of thought to the weather. If you don't have the right tires on your car when you're running in the rain or on a hot day, you might as well stay home and play Donkey Kong."

She went on, "Another problem with marrying a pit man. He's always looking for ways to cool the fuel before it reaches the combustion chamber. You could say axle grease broke up our marriage."

Hands went up. Voices asked her to elaborate on the axle grease.

Maxine said, "Your pit man spends hours thinning the grease, trying to come up with a lighter lubricant to cut down on friction. One day I asked Joe Ed why he didn't spread that axle grease on my body, see if it turned me on. He had the audacity to say that if he had any axle grease to spare, he'd use it on Lisa Ann Grimes—she never raised hell about nothing."

She said, "It's a big scene in the movie the day I kicked Joe Ed in his brass and told him he'd blocked off my radiator for the last time. Don't ask me what the real Joe Ed is doing these days, or where he is. He's out of my life. And I've sent Eugene off to a foster home. The little snaggletooth snot almost burned down our mobile home smoking a cigar. He'll make a good convict someday."

Notes on Eugene were scribbled throughout the room.

Somebody asked who plays Joe Ed in the movie.

She said, "You know, I can't think of his name, but his face is familiar. He's one of those actors who's not a leading man but you see him so many times on the screen you feel like he's kin."

Maxine finished off her longneck Bud and said, "If you boys have everything you need, let's get after some of this cuisine Junior's laid out for us on the buffet table. I believe I see some queso to dip and his special chili poured over the Frito scoops."

She thanked everyone for coming, and said, "By the way, I've developed an interest in Dirt Bike Racing. I'm working with Freddie Drake on a treatment for a movie about it. Now Dirt Bike. There's a sport where you find out pretty quick who the real men are."

We applauded her and slid out of our chairs.

Maxine said, "One last thing. I want all of you to know I'm a happy single girl again. And I'll tell you this. Living the life of a single girl is a damn sight easier when you're not married."

Our Lives in Their Hands

TRYING TO STAY ALIVE in your own automobile today has become a treacherous sport. More often than not I find myself saying, "Why do I have to risk death because I want to hop in my car and go buy a dozen eggs?"

I have a list of people who are intent on trying to kill me—but never themselves—at any hour of the day and night when they're seated behind the wheel of a moving vehicle. The prime culprits are:

Your Texting Sap. Your Pickup Maniac. Your Teenage Jerk. Your Drunken Fool. Your Happy Hour Lunatic. Your Red Car Moron.

I'll take them one at a time.

Those who love to text while driving firmly believe they have urgent news to relate to friends or relatives.

"Hi. Central Bakery was out of the sourdough bread. I'm pulling off the freeway now and will try Mrs. Simpson's. I need to pick up something from Ed's Cleaners. Can't remember what it is, but I'll stop anyhow. I want to drop by the taco wagon in the park, but I might get caught in going-home traffic. I don't think you want peppers in your bean and cheese burrito, but text me back if I'm wrong. Saw Janet in her new Cadillac. Makes me want one. Uh-oh. Nearly missed my turn."

Nobody is in as big of a hurry as the maniac in the pickup. He likes to see how many ambers he can beat in a single day. His normal speed is seventy-five miles an hour in the city. Over a hundred on the loop.

Here's a life-saving tip for you. When you're stopped at an intersection, wait at least five seconds to go after the light turns green. Do this no matter how many impatient people behind you are honking their horns. The pickup guy trying to beat an amber can come out of nowhere and broadside you—and do it on the driver's side. Need I say more?

THE TEENAGE JERK is a menace every moment he or she is at the wheel. They are more of a threat if their parents are well-to-do. The teenager knows that no matter how many people he or she may kill or injure in a wreck or a hit-and-run, Mom and Dad will buy a judge and keep them out of jail. And they won't even be grounded.

The teenager's motto is: "Dummies ought to know to stay out of my way when I want to go somewhere."

DRUNKEN FOOLS at the wheel have proven over time that they have an uncanny sense of how to do something no sober or sane person would even try.

Without thinking about it, the drunk somehow has this knack for knowing how to enter and drive the wrong way on a divided freeway.

Most motorists could look for a lifetime and never figure out how to find the wrong-way entrance on a freeway. But we too often read about an accident that happened because a drunken fool miraculously managed to wind up going the wrong way on 20 East or 30 West. At the crash scene, a sheriff's deputy will say, "You couldn't manage to put a car where that vehicle was found if you had a crane to lift it up and drop it there."

THE HAPPY HOUR lunatic is in as big a hurry as the pickup maniac.

If it's a guy, he'll pretend he's in a drag race to reach Paula's Lounge in time for two cocktails, a feel-up, and some kisses with his girlfriend Cheryl before he goes home to his pregnant wife.

If it's a babe, she'll be in the same hurry to spend an intimate hour with her boss, the lawyer, before he goes home to his wife and four children.

THE RED CAR MORON is as dangerous as any of the others. Maybe more so. If you think about all the times a vehicle has tailgated you, drafted you, slipstreamed you, passed you on the right, and never—*never* in history—used a turn signal, it's nearly always a moron in a red car.

Why would anyone own a red car unless they're trying to show their loyalty to the Alabama Crimson Tide, Georgia Bulldogs, Oklahoma Sooners, Nebraska Cornhuskers, or Arkansas Razorbacks?

Drivers of red cars should be barred from everything except crashing into other red cars.

"Officer, I don't know what happened. I was only reading a text while I was trying to light a cigarette and change the radio station, but all of a sudden I wound up in this ditch with that other car."

Horses and Players

AS A CASUAL FAN of horse racing in the strictest sense, the main thing I've noticed through the years is that the bonnets on the ladies in the grandstands have grown larger and sillier.

Other than that, I'm like any other average sports fan where the thoroughbreds are concerned. I watch the Triple Crown races on TV. Every big sports event is of interest to me.

There are exceptions. Bungee jumping off the top of the Empire State Building is one. Snorkeling with piranhas in the Amazon is two. Any other X Game you care to mention will be included.

With the thoroughbreds, however, it's safe to say that I've been to race tracks fewer times than I've been to Cleveland. There was my only visit to Churchill Downs for a Kentucky Derby. Five other occasions would be the Belmont Stakes I attended when I was living in Manhattan and was invited by friends to loiter in the comforts of the Jockey Club. I went up to Saratoga twice for the Travers. The rest would be drop-ins on Agua Caliente, when it was a horse track, along with Del Mar, Ruidoso Downs, and Lone Star Park.

That kind of shoddy attendance may explain why I'm 0-for-winner.

It might also have something to do with my habit of betting long shots to Win Only. What's the point otherwise?

I've never been a guy who'd bet the heavy favorite so I could brag that I had him when I strolled to the window to collect the $4.20 profit.

I came close once. It was on my one trip to Churchill Downs. Not to cover the Derby but for fun and frolic at the invitation of TV pals at CBS. This was 1969, the year Bill Hartack won his fifth Derby on Majestic Prince. I bet the second favorite, Arts and Letters.

The name of that chestnut colt was calling to me. Arts and Letters. It was my profession, after all. I'd read thick novels in college. Tried to, anyhow. The signs were everywhere. If you'd tied me down in a dentist's chair, I'd have said, "Keep drilling, I feel lucky."

Arts and Letters did run a valiant race. He finished second. Naturally I'd bet him to Win Only.

FOR A NONCHALANT FAN of the sport, I can look back with amazement that I was present for two immortal events at the Belmont.

One was in 1973 when Secretariat wrapped up the first Triple Crown in twenty-five years. He had more than a "safe trip," as they say in the saddling ring. He was the Lock of Eternity, and ran like it.

Big Red, as he was known, surely the greatest thoroughbred in history, set a world record for the mile and a half and won by thirty-one lengths that day. Ron Turcotte, his pilot, rode the stirrups the whole trip, never giving a thought to applying the whip to Secretariat's rump. Big Red just liked to outrun other horses.

I may have been the only person in the crowd of seventy thousand who didn't buy a $2 win ticket on him to keep as a souvenir.

Didn't matter. I wound up with one anyhow. My good friend Danny Lavezzo, the owner of P. J. Clarke's, had bought a healthy stack of them that afternoon, and as the days followed Danny handed them out to loyalists who dropped by Clarke's in the evenings, to "pick up the mail," we joked.

Most horse players aren't that thoughtful.

The other time was in '78. This was the day that the Belmont Stakes offered up the classic duel between Affirmed and Alydar, the most exciting horse race in the annals of heart attacks.

My wife and I and several friends were there to cheer for Affirmed to wrap up the Triple Crown—and to root for a book deal.

A book deal? True.

The late Pete Axthelm of *Newsweek*, a good friend and hang-out companion, had a publishing deal hinging on the result. Affirmed was ridden by Steve Cauthen, the teenage jockey, and a major publisher would make a book deal with Pete about Cauthen if the kid completed the Triple Crown. The kid piloting Affirmed had barely managed to fight off Alydar in both the Derby and Preakness.

We limbered up with pre-race cocktails in the Jockey Club and were well in the mood to join in the singing of "The Sidewalks of New York" when the horses came on the track. "Sidewalks" was still the Belmont theme at the time.

But right now our group was singing lyrics to the theme that we made up as we went along. None of us had personally known a Mamie O'Rourke. We sang:

East Side, West Side,
Going out for fun.
Start with cocktails at Toots's,
Move on to 21.
Guys and dolls together,
Elaine's to P. J. Clarke.
Keep the good times rolling
On The Sidewalks of New York.

Twenty years later a marketing genius changed the Belmont theme to Sinatra's recording of "New York, New York" despite the fact that you could hear it five times a day on any radio station in the Metropolitan area.

But now came the race.

The kid quickly took Affirmed to the lead on the rail. The more mature jockey, Jorge Velasquez, laid off with Alydar until the long backstretch. That's when he pulled Alydar up to Affirmed's right hip. From the far turn through the home stretch and all the way to the finish line, they galloped side by side, stride for stride, whip for whip. If Alydar nudged ahead, Affirmed would find another gear.

Affirmed won that Belmont—and the book deal—by a nostril.

And all I knew was, I didn't need to see another horse race the rest of my days. It had just got done.

Athletes of the Air

TODAY'S YOUTH might be surprised to learn that there was once a time in this country when people pointed at airplanes if they looked up and saw one. It's rumored they still do this in parts of the South, although I can't swear to it personally. But I do know that America's fascination with flight was responsible for "the Golden Age of Air Racing."

Air racing?

You mean like people climbed into cockpits of airplanes, cranked up, took off, and raced each other around a course of pylons to see who could win or get killed first?

Exactly.

It happened when the Cleveland National Air Races were held annually from 1929 through 1939 over a ten-day period that concluded on Labor Day weekend. The sport captured the attention of citizens around the globe throughout those eleven years. The event more or less ended when it was canceled during World War II and suffered a loss of interest afterward because the aircraft propeller had gone the way of the icebox.

Among the happenings at Cleveland Municipal Airport were exhibitions of stunt flying, wing-walking, dogfights, parachuting, and enough plane crashes to satisfy the ghouls in the crowd. But it included two hugely popular events, the Thompson Trophy Race and the Bendix Trophy Race. Their pilots were looked upon as the bravest of athletes. The races often drew crowds in Cleveland that reached 150,000 in a single day.

The world had been fascinated with aviation since "the Great War," when flying aces like Captain Eddie Rickenbacker in his Spad and the Red Baron, Manfred von Richthofen, in his Fokker were dogfighting against their enemies in the skies over France.

Following that, Americans became more fascinated with flight. They were instantly enthralled with the barnstormers and stunt flyers who populated the clouds, and next by two "pioneers of aviation" who achieved worldwide fame by flying solo across the Atlantic Ocean.

Those pioneers were Charles "Lucky Lindy" Lindbergh and Amelia "Lady Lindy" Earhart, who became "America's Sweetheart of the Air." The fetching Amelia had only to grin in order to make a headline or become a spread in the rotogravure section of your Sunday newspaper.

There were other notable lady flyers. Among the most prominent were Louise Thaden, who was setting speed, altitude, and endurance records, and Blanche Noyes, Pancho Barnes, and Laura Ingalls. But none had Amelia's star quality.

WHEN THE AERIAL SHOW started in Cleveland in '29, it featured the Bendix and Thompson races along with a Women's Air Derby, a coast-to-coast contest for lady aviators, Santa Monica to Cleveland. Will Rogers nicknamed it "the Powder Puff Derby." His words alone didn't harm its publicity one bit.

Louise Thaden won the race in a time of twenty hours and nineteen minutes. Amelia Earhart finished third—and stomped around on the landing strip in a fury due to the oversight that her plane hadn't been equipped with enough horsepower in the first place.

Women weren't permitted to enter the Bendix Trophy Race for the first five years of its existence. But when they did, in 1936, they dominated it. Louise Thaden in her bi-wing Beechcraft, with Blanche Noyes for a copilot, won the event in a little under fifteen hours. She finished one hour ahead of Laura Ingalls.

"What a surprise," Louise said. "I thought we'd be the cow's tail."

She had reason to think this. Amelia Earhart was the big favorite in her revolutionary single-wing Lockheed Electra with the accomplished Helen Richey for a co-pilot. But the two ladies were nearly killed when the escape hatch on the Electra's cockpit blew off and almost sucked them into space. They managed to grab the hatch and desperately hold onto it with rags until Amelia could land for a fuel stop in Kansas City. But they lost valuable time repairing the hatch with wires, and finished fifth.

That episode may have been an omen. A year later, while attempting to become the first woman to circle the globe, Amelia perished in the effort. Her radio lost communication with the world and her plane disappeared over the central Pacific, halfway between Hawaii and Australia. It's still debated as to whether she crashed into the sea or on Howland Island, an uninhabited chunk of coral. All of America mourned the tragedy.

THE FIRST OFFICIAL WINNER of the Bendix in 1931 was a fellow named Jimmy Doolittle. He turned out to be the same Col. James Doolittle who trained and led the squad of sixteen B-25s that took off from the USS *Hornet*, part of Admiral Halsey's Task Force, to make the surprise bombing raid on Tokyo in '42.

But the flyer who became the brightest star of the Cleveland air show was a swashbuckling Hollywood stunt flyer named Roscoe Turner. He won the Thompson Trophy Race three times—it came with a hefty cash prize and a large work-of-art trophy—and, more importantly, he lived to tell about it. The Thompson race was the premier attraction in Cleveland. The fans could actually see most of the race from the grandstands.

This exhilarating competition was a thirty-lap race covering ten miles in which the flyers took off simultaneously and circled a rectangular course of five fifty-foot pylons making sharp turns at close range and going 280 miles an hour while passing each other back and forth—or trying to.

One of the surviving competitors remarked, "The hardest part was reaching the first pylon without getting killed."

Having won the Bendix trophy in 1933, Roscoe Turner won the Thompson Trophy Race in '34, '38, and '39 in his juiced-up single-wing Turner RT Meteor, an aircraft of gleaming silver with wheel spats. He was once timed in one lap of the Thompson race at 299 miles per hour.

Roscoe parlayed his triumphs into a radio show and film parts, and books were written about him, one of which labeled him "The Throttle Bendin' Devil." When he wasn't racing, he set transcontinental speed records, earned the Distinguished Flying Cross, adopted a pet lion as a cub—named him Gilmore—took the lion with him on highly-publicized flights, promoted passenger air travel, lived in Beverly Hills with his first wife Caroline, and hobnobbed with movie stars.

THE POPULARITY of the Cleveland races undoubtedly encouraged Hollywood to grind out more airplane movies. The trend had begun with the silent *Wings,* starring Clara Bow and Richard Arlen, and by Howard Hughes's *Hell's Angels,* with Ben Lyon and Jean Harlow.

Those epics were followed by a spate of films in which happy-go-lucky pilots did loop-de-loops and flew the mail through blizzards, wise-cracking every moment, but often not making it back to the ground alive.

These were movies where the leading actors had role names like Dizzy and Tex, and the supporting actors were called Sparks and Slugger. Two of the films are considered classics: *Ceiling Zero* with James Cagney and Pat O'Brien, and *Only Angels Have Wings* with Cary Grant, Jean Arthur, and Rita Hayworth.

"Don't try to land in this soup, Dizzy!"

"It's okay, Tex. I think I see an opening."

One of my personal favorites was *Tail Spin,* obviously inspired by the Powder Puff Derby. In *Tail Spin* the actress Constance Bennett, portraying a socialite turned aviator, and Alice Faye, portraying a waitress turned aviator, have a cat fight in the skies over a leading man nobody's heard of since.

As in *Tail Spin,* part of the charm of airplane movies that starred chicks was Hollywood insisting that they have appropriate role names like Trixie, Honey, Babe, and Alabama.

IT'S NO WONDER that the combination of Hollywood and a fearless pilot like Roscoe Turner made a kid want to put on an aviator's cap and goggles and twirl a white scarf around his neck when he went to see an airplane movie.

It comes close to astounding nowadays to think back and realize that in 1939 there would have been no way any of those daredevils of flight could imagine men walking on the moon only thirty years later.

Thirty years?

Hell, it was only thirty years ago that Madonna foisted herself on mankind.

Food Fight

IN MY LIFETIME I could never have imagined that I would see the simple joy of dining become a contact sport. But that's what has taken place since the millennium ushered in these legions of precious chefs who are determined to stamp out any food that we know, enjoy, or, for that matter, recognize.

If we don't stop these ominous clowns before they outnumber the reliable cooks in our society, we aren't likely to have traditional Thanksgiving and Christmas dinners to rely on. Instead we'll be treated to:

A nice roasted flamingo accented with kiwi, spinach in the cornbread dressing, sardines in the giblet gravy, applesauce in the mashed potatoes, raisins in the sweet potatoes, and southern green beans swimming in Chanel perfume.

I grew up on the food everybody's grandmother cooked.

I never ate a peanut butter and carambola sandwich, okay?

More food eaters need to become as angry as I am and join in the battle. We have to fight this absurd trend or an average meal at our neighborhood café will consist of mesquite-grilled raccoon on a bed of cranberry sauce with a baked cricket salad. And dessert? A pineapple tamale or a tomato snow cone.

My burning question to a precious chef is: why does my entree have to look like a sunset over Tahiti?

I want food, not a photo op.

I noticed what was happening to food long before the millennium arrived. It was when the country found itself under siege from a plethora of outrageously expensive restaurants where the specialty of the evening was a Brussels sprout nuzzling up to a bleeding squab.

I was talked into dining at this kind of joint by friends, although I was suspicious of the name to begin with. The Crocheted Aardvark.

My first bite of the appetizer proved that my fear was real.

"What is *this*?" I asked around the table irritably.

"Calamari," somebody said.

"It looks like a French fry."

"It's squid."

"It's *what*?"

"Squid. Give it a chance."

"Squid is an octopus. They eat submarines!"

The nearest disinfectant was my glass of scotch and water. I poured it down my neck, and ordered two backups.

It took less than another minute for me to launch into a *Hamlet* soliloquy.

I said, "Do you take me for a guy who drinks skim milk? Food is brown and tan. Okay, it's orange if we're talking about cheese. Maroon if it's pinto beans. You want Swiss on your cheeseburger, move to California. Let joggers eat hummus. Let a Frenchman take an hour to croque your noisette. Spaghetti Bolognese is the only pasta. The corned beef sandwich made America great. Hash browns helped. So did beef stew. Who needs a cocktail?"

Nobody. I'd almost cleared the room.

Half of the people at the table departed before I took out a notepad and made a list of things the precious chefs can be charged with as punishable crimes in my administration.

Public hanging for:

> *Making cornbread with sugar in it.*
> *Liver in any form.*
> *Veggie burgers*
> *Tripe and onions.*
> *Trout tacos.*
> *All abnormal tacos.*
> *A dish so spicy its makes your armpits glow.*
> *Quail eggs benedict on lemon biscuits.*
> *Herring wrap.*
> *Sushi.*

Tongue.
Thinking Navy beans are blue.

Lethal injection for:

Tortilla soup—it's all over for that.
Calling it barbecue when it doesn't come from Texas.
Goat cheese.
Eggplant.
Okra.
Turkey sausage.
Turkey chili.
A hotdog wiener that's made out of turkey and chicken.
Fruit on a pizza.
Carrot cake.
Foam.
Southern fried chicken cooked in a batter that smells like fish.
Sweetbreads. They're throats, for Christ sake.

Life without parole for:

Blackened anything—it's all over for that, too.
Duck fajitas.
Fajitas.
Tofu.
Squash.
Cauliflower.
Yogurt.
Ostrich and vegetable gelatin.
Avocado toast.
Coconut water.
Seaweed.
The egg white omelet.
Plopping my steak down on top of the mashed potatoes.

IT'LL BE A LONG, vicious fight with the precious chefs, who keep multiplying and gaining the support of the anorexic people. But my ankles are taped, I've rubbed on the eye black, I'm ready.

The Mother of
Sports Quizzes

AN INDIVIDUAL GAME I indulge in from time to time is creating quizzes that ask you to answer many of the most nagging questions that haunt today's sports world. This one is challenging, but at least you won't have to know what a gnu is, as in crosswords. Here we go:

How many schools are currently in the Big 10 Conference?

Fourteen
Nine
Twelve

The NFL commissioner has determined that one of these players has deflated the most footballs in the game's history:

William "Refrigerator" Perry
Gene "Big Daddy" Lipscomb
"Concrete Charley" Bednarik

Which of these swimmers least reminds you of Michael Phelps?

Esther Williams
Ryan Lochte
Das Boot

Pinstripes were first worn by . . .

The New York Yankees
Bjorn Borg
Al Capone

Tom Brady won more Super Bowls than . . .

> Joe Montana
> Terry Bradshaw
> considerably more than Tony Romo

The infield fly rule is . . .

> part of the dress code at stock car races
> helpful in sky diving
> a baseball rule only two living sportswriters can explain

Drop volley is . . .

> a ski trail in Aspen
> a Polynesian cocktail
> something a rock star does on the stage

Yogi Berra has more World Series rings (ten) than . . .

> Joe DiMaggio (nine)
> Lou Gehrig (eight)
> That's not possible, is it?

The four most endearing college bowl games are . . .

> Rose, Sugar, Orange, Cotton
> Fiesta, Peach, Liberty, Sun
> Idaho Potato, Bad Boys Mowers, Taxslayer, Foster Farms

The smallest world heavyweight boxing champion was . . .

> Tommy Burns
> Rocky Marciano
> Sylvester Stallone

Fanny Blankers-Koen was . . .

> "The Flying Housewife" from Holland who won four gold medals
> in track at the '48 Summer Olympics
> A board game
> Luftwaffe code in World War II for "Let's do Rotterdam again."

"No mas" was uttered by . . .

> Benito Mussolini
> Muammar Gaddafi
> Roberto Duran

Pepper Martin, the St. Louis Cardinal Hall of Famer, was known as . . .

"The Wild Bull of the Pampas"
"The Wild Hoss of the Plains"
"The Wild Horse of the Osage"

Actually "The Wild Bull of the Pampas" was . . .

Primo Carnera
Oscar Bonavena
Luis Firpo

The greatest college football team that played both ways was . . .

1930—Notre Dame (10-0, Marchy Schwartz)
1938—TCU (11-0, Davey O'Brien)
1940—Michigan (7-1, Tom Harmon)

The greatest college football team under platoon rules was . . .

1969—Texas (11-0, James Street)
1972—USC (12-0, Anthony Davis)
1995—Nebraska (12-0, Tommie Frazier)

The greatest NFL team of all time is . . .

1972—Miami Dolphins (14-0, Bob Griese, Larry Csonka)
1962—Green Bay Packers (13-1, Bart Starr, Paul Hornung)
1977—Dallas Cowboys (12-2, Roger Staubach, Tony Dorsett)

The man who fixed the 1919 World Series was . . .

Dutch Schultz
Legs Diamond
Arnold Rothstein

Man o' War's only loss in twenty-one races was to a horse named . . .

Sir Barton
Regret
Upset

The greatest female athlete of all time is still . . .

Babe Didrikson Zaharias
Jackie Joyner-Kersee
Bruce Jenner

The sport that's hardest for normal people to understand is . . .

Lacrosse
Cricket
jai alai

Baseball spring training is . . .

necessary for ball clubs to get in shape
necessary for managers to work on their golf games
a paid vacation for baseball writers

Stanford's Hank Luisetti invented . . .

the wireless
the telephone
the one-hand push shot in basketball

Bobby Charlton was . . .

one of the original Beatles
one of the original Stones
one of England's greatest soccer stars

The fifth member of basketball's original "Dream Team" with Michael, Magic, Bird, and Barclay was . . .

Every
Body
Else

Lance Armstrong sold more bikes worldwide than . . .

The Tour de France
Dick's Sporting Goods
The US Anti-Doping Agency

The Summer Olympics of 2024 will be held . . .

in the Sirharaja Rain Forest of Sri Lanka
on Krakatoa during another volcanic eruption
in Pyongyang, North Korea, during a raid by US B-1B bombers
    and F-35 fighter jets

What Major League manager said, "That's what baseball do."

Casey Stengel

Sparky Anderson
Ron Washington

Who would have won the Heisman Trophy if it had originated in 1924?

Red Grange
One of the Four Horsemen at Notre Dame
Grantland Rice

The most deserving player who DID NOT win the Heisman was . . .

Peyton Manning at Tennessee
Deshaun Watson at Clemson
Both

The only college football coach to win a national championship at three different universities was . . .

Urban Meyer
Bear Bryant
Howard Jones

Which of these horses is most loved?

Secretariat
Seabiscuit
Trigger

In the heyday of Roller Derby, the most popular star was . . .

Midge (Toughie) Brasuhn
Ann Calvello
Gerry Murray

Which of these three sets of drivers won the Indy 500 four times?

Richard Petty, Dale Earnhardt Sr., Jimmie Johnson
A. J. Foyt, Al Unser Sr., Rick Mears
Steve McQueen, James Garner, Paul Newman

Cal's Vic Bottari was . . .

"The San Berdoo Bearcat"
"The Melrose Cannonball"
"The Vallejo Venetian"

Tennessee Coach Pat Summitt's most-used remark to one of her weepy basketball players was . . .

"Stay out of my sight."
"Why did I recruit you?"
"Toughen up, buttercup."

The best Hollywood actor who played football in college was . . .

John Wayne at USC
Burt Reynolds at Florida State
Tommy Lee Jones at Harvard

Before Detroit's Kenny McLain won thirty-one games in '68, the last pitcher to win thirty in a season was . . .

Lefty Grove with Red Sox
Bob Feller with the Indians
Dizzy Dean with the Cardinals

What pitcher at his peak would you put on the mound for your life?

Sandy Koufax
Bob Gibson
Nolan Ryan

The worst result in sports history was . . .

Unknown Jack Fleck beating Ben Hogan in the U.S. Open playoff of '55
Jack Dempsey getting robbed from regaining the world heavyweight boxing title by "the Long Count" on Gene Tunney in 1927
Jockey Willie Shoemaker misjudging the finish line and standing up in the irons on Gallant Man to lose the '57 Kentucky Derby by a nose to Bill Hartack on Iron Liege

After Jackie Robinson joined the Brooklyn Dodgers in the National League, the first black player taken into the American League was . . .

Larry Doby
Satchel Paige
Elston Howard

Which of these three quarterbacks won the most NFL championships before the Super Bowl existed?

> Otto Graham of the Cleveland Browns
> Arnie Herber of the Green Bay Packers
> Sid Luckman of the Chicago Bears

Who said, "Kill, kill . . . kill for the love of killing"?

> Geno Auriemma to his UConn girls before every game
> Coach John Heisman in 1916 to his Georgia Tech team while it was
>   beating Cumberland by 222 to 0
> Eduardo Ciannelli portraying the evil guru in *Gunga Din*

What did sportswriter Jimmy Cannon blurt out at ringside when Sonny Liston took a dive in the first round from Ali's "phantom punch"?

> "My pocket's been picked!"
> "Gimme a break!"
> "You gotta be kidding!"

Any baseball writer who votes to keep Pete Rose out of the Hall of Fame must never have . . .

> missed a Sunday in church
> told a lie
> fudged on his income tax

Golf's most absorbing era was . . .

> Ben Hogan, Byron Nelson, Sam Snead
> Jack Nicklaus, Arnold Palmer, Gary Player
> Tiger, Elin, Raychel, Jamie, Mindy, Holly

America's first lady to win the Olympic gold medal in figure skating was . . .

> Peggy Fleming
> Tenley Albright
> Jennifer Aniston

The best sports movie ever made is . . .

> *Slap Shot*
> *Chariots of Fire*
> *Bull Durham*

Bat Masterson, a gunfighter in the Old West, eventually became . . .

a dead gunfighter in the Old West
a lawman in Dodge City
a sports columnist for the *New York Morning Telegraph*

Which one of these legendary athletes said, "If you can't drink and drive, how come most bars have parking lots?"

Mickey Mantle
Babe Ruth
Bobby Layne

The Last Word—
Words, I Mean

SOME MEMBER of the intelligentsia has said that no sport is worthwhile unless it has a literature. But I say every sport is worthwhile to one group or another. It's just that certain sports have a more obscure literature than others.

For instance, is it bowling's fault that so few people read *A Farewell to Akron* by Ernie Henderson?

I went in the diner to get some eggs.

A waitress called out, "Frederick's here, Catherine. Start crackin' 'em"

The waitress turned to me. "How many today?"

"Six basted."

She brought scrambled.

"You brought scrambled," I said.

"Catherine don't know about basted," the waitress said.

I ate the eggs even though they were not good and true and strong. I was hungry. But I knew it was time to cut Catherine loose. She hadn't rolled a strike in two weeks. I didn't even wave at the kitchen window. I just ducked out the door and rolled up the pack of smokes in the sleeve of my T-shirt and walked back to my truck in the rain.

Cycling takes its share of abuse, particularly if you're talking about the substance kind that goes with every racer who slips on the yellow jersey. Still, it's unfortunate that more people haven't discovered *Mein Schwinn* by Heinz von Gertler.

Adolf and Eva churn their bikes to the top of the hill and stop to take in the scenery.

"Where are we?" Eva asks.

"Austria. It's mine now."

"Wonderful. Where to next, big guy?"

"I want to take a look at Poland. See what's left."

"I want to see France. Why do you think I brought my camera?"

"In due time. I want to stop in Poland and Belgium for a moment."

"What's in Belgium?"

"A few Gestapo friends. Other than that, not much."

"Let's get it out of the way, then."

"Calm down, strudel. I want to enjoy every stop . . . Poland . . . Belgium . . . France . . . the Netherlands . . . Luxembourg . . . Romania . . . "

"I wish we could go to Russia."

Adolf does a line of coke, and says, "Russia? Why not?"

Gymnastics is only popular during the Olympics, but this would not be the case if Irene Denison's *Out of Amarillo* had attracted more readers.

I had a farm in Amarillo. It was near a row of worthless turbine windmills and a Dairy Queen. You want to talk about back flips, vaults, cartwheels, and floor exercises? You should have seen me the day I left that place for good.

Fencing has never been as popular as it should be, even though it dates back to the days when duels were fought to the death. It would help if more people read John le Éclair's *Tinker, Tailor, Soldier, Foil, Epee, Sabre.*

"Why, Bill?"

George had gone to visit Bill in his cell.

"Why?" said Bill. "God, why not? I quite hate America, you see."

"What has America done to you?"

"They cheated me out of the gold medal, or have you forgotten?"

"But Bill," George said. "That was no reason to send poor Jim Fido into Czechoslovakia. Jim isn't even an American. You had to know Jim would be more than touched, nicked, and pin-pricked by those swordsmen."

"I got him back, didn't I?"

"Yes . . . in parts. That was good of you."

THERE IS ANOTHER SAYING that goes, "The smaller the ball, the better the literature." But if you believe that nonsense, you must think ping pong has a better literature than football, in which case I may have to arrange an intervention.

Other sports books have reached the marketplace that deserve attention. I'm pleased to present these excerpts from the most promising batch, although some don't involve a ball of any size.

From *Everything You Want to Know About Distance Running but Are Afraid to Ask an Algerian,* by Kassim Farouk with Dick Sullivan.

"I stole the jewels and ran. That was the start of it."

From *Downtown Danny Blake,* by Danny Blake with Marv Turner.

"I got the bat. I got the glove. I got the rings. I got the broads. Who wouldn't want to be me?"

From *Hold Your Fire: Confessions of an NFL Referee,* by Fred Warrington with Joanne Richards.

"My wife enjoys betting on games, so around the house you hear a lot of talk about judgment calls."

From *Screaming Headphones: My Life as a Head Coach with the Worst Offensive Coordinator in College Football,* by Duke Frank with Spike Herbert.

"No gain up the middle. Short side option, no gain. Another short-side option, no gain. Punt. Ask me if I got tired of having that moron on my staff."

From *Layin' Wood on Their Ass: The Life of Mad Dog Gruder, a Twelve-Year All-Pro Linebacker in the NFL,* by Mad Dog Gruder with Chuck Lance.

"The Cowboys. The Giants. The Packers. The Steelers. All the others. Every Sunday. Sometimes Monday night. I'm there. It's what I do. What do you do? You watch me. That's what you do."

From *The Agatha and the Ecstasy,* by Stud Springer with Meg Adams.

"Nobody loved mixed doubles more than Agatha Birch. We were partners through ten Wimbledons, a period that covered five divorces—three of hers, two of mine. But one day she met Ludvig, and . . . "

From *A View from Above the Rim,* by Tomsk Stepanov with Reggie York.

"In Russia they make fun of boy seven foot tall and baldheaded. Now it is I who laugh. In United States I discover burger. No more eat cucumbers."

From *Chukker to Chukker,* by Hunt Faircloth III with Lydia Faircloth.

"It's not easy to become a 10-goal player when you're sent off to college with only twelve polo ponies."

From *I Crewed on Avenger,* by Skip Hancock with Buzz Taylor.

"They say the America's Cup is like watching paint grow. I mean dry. People say this because they've never accidentally fallen overboard and been forced to swim for it. We were killing New Zealand that day when . . . "

From *Riders Up!,* by Jacinto Zapata with Blake Winters.

"I heet de horse."

From *Applaud This!* by Jake Stroker with Roy Harper.

"I want to thank everybody who helped me succeed on the PGA Tour, but I can't think of nobody who did that much."

From *Harpoon Hazel*, by Hazel Burris with Patsy Clayton.

"They said no woman could throw a javelin that far—it was physically impossible. I'm glad the ambulance arrived in time to rush the official to the hospital where his life was saved. But he can't say I didn't keep waving at him to back up . . . back up."

From *Speed Sawyer's Last Race* by Speed Sawyer with Mark Walters.

"They hollered in my ear to use my right foot and go for it. So I did. But a minute later I had a choice to make. Hit the wall or hit the car in front of me. I chose the car. Which turned out to be three cars. Well, four, counting mine. And the next thing I knew . . ."

From *Punchy*, by Irish Kid Callahan, the Shamrock Spider, as told to Sean O'Hearn.

"I shudda seen the shot comin' when the beaner throwed it."

From *Brews, Chips, and Sofas: America's Preoccupation with Sports on TV*, by Harvard Professor Jerome King and Yale Professor Hiram Underwood.

"In the beginning there was the universe, though not necessarily."

ABOUT THE AUTHOR

DAN JENKINS is an award-winning sportswriter and best-selling novelist whose career spans seven decades. He is the author of twenty-three books—twelve novels and eleven works of non-fiction. After fifteen years of writing for newspapers in Fort Worth and Dallas, Jenkins became nationally known for his stories in *Sports Illustrated* over a period of twenty-five years, for his stint as a sports columnist for *Playboy*, and for his essays, features, and tweets in *Golf Digest*. After thirty years of living in New York City, Jenkins and his wife June returned to Fort Worth.

Three of his novels, *Semi-Tough, Baja Oklahoma,* and *Dead Solid Perfect* have been made into movies. He is one of only four writers who have been inducted into the World Golf Hall of Fame. He has also been inducted into the National Sportscasters and Sportswriters Hall of Fame, the Texas Sports Hall of Fame, the Texas Golf Hall of Fame, and the TCU Lettermen's Hall of Fame. For a career of excellence in sportswriting, Jenkins has received the Red Smith Award, the Ring Lardner Award, the PEN Award, the Lifetime Achievement Award from the PGA of America, and many other honors. His daughter, Sally Jenkins, a best-selling author and prize-winning sports columnist for the *Washington Post*, calls the office in his home "the walls that ate Fort Worth."

In 2017, he was honored when the press box in TCU's Amon G. Carter Stadium was named the Dan Jenkins Press Box, and again when the University of Texas in Austin created the Dan Jenkins Medal to be awarded annually to the country's outstanding sportswriter, as selected by a national panel of sports journalists.